SHAPE UP

BY O. Quentin Hyder, M.D.

The Christian's Handbook of Psychiatry
The People You Live With
Shape Up

SHAPE UP

O. Quentin Hyder, M.D.

Fleming H. Revell Company
Old Tappan, New Jersey

Appendix L reprinted with permission: condensed from "Too Young to Die: The Case for Staying Healthy and Alive Through Preventive Medicine" by Donald R. Germann, M.D. Published by Farnsworth Publishing Company, Inc. Copyrighted, 1974. $9.95. The book can be purchased from the company at 78 Randall Avenue, Rockville Centre, New York 11570.

Appendix I from THE COMPLETE BOOK OF RUNNING, by James F. Fixx. Copyright © 1977 by James F. Fixx. Reprinted by permission of Random House, Inc.

Table, "The Stress of Adjusting to Change," in THE RELAXATION RESPONSE by Herbert Benson, M.D. Copyright © 1975 by William Morrow & Company, Inc. By permission of the publisher.

"Caloric Cost of Running" chart reprinted with permission from Jog, Run, Race, published by World Publications, Inc.

Line drawings in chapter 13 are by Peter Harrison.

Cartoons in chapters 1 and 12 are by Michael Witte.

Jogging photographs are by L. Charles Carr, Ph.D.

The squash photograph is by Robert H. Lehmann.

Scripture quotations not otherwise identified are from the King James Version of the Bible.

Scripture quotations identified NEB are from The New English Bible. © The Delegates of the Oxford University Press and the Syndics of the Cambridge University Press, 1961 and 1970. Reprinted by permission.

Library of Congress Cataloging in Publication Data

Hyder, O. Quentin, 1930–
    Shape up.

    Bibliography: p.
    1. Health.   2. Christian life—1960–   I. Title.
RA776.5.H93   613   78-11765
ISBN 0-8007-0975-6

TO
the memory of my father,
Dr. Roland I. Hyder,
Christian, physician, sportsman.
(1903–1975)

Contents

Appendices

Acknowledgments

IN MY FIRST TWO BOOKS I acknowledged the men and women who had most influenced me both in my professional career as a physician and psychiatrist and in my personal spiritual growth as a Christian. Here I wish to mention those who have most helped me to develop a balanced attitude toward the importance of physical well-being as an integral part of total health.

Again I remember my parents first. My father, the late Dr. Roland I. Hyder, himself in youth a boxer, cross-country runner, cricketer, and later a low-handicap golfer, strongly encouraged me in all my sporting endeavors as I was going through school.

My mother, also a physician, gave me for my twenty-first birthday the cost of having lessons to fly small, single-engined aircraft, as she herself did. She also not only encouraged me to study the workings of the body by going to medical school and constantly influenced me to pursue intellectual activities, but she herself, as a retired physician, went back to college and obtained a second Bachelor's degree fifty years after her first, at the age of seventy-two. She also infused into me a little of her great compassion and concern for people going through physical or emotional suffering.

Roger Bannister, who was a medical student in London at the same time that I was, inspired me to believe that realistic goals *are* attainable, when he ran the first ever sub-four-minute mile.

More recently I want to thank very specially my much-admired friend Peter Yaman, who at fifty looks thirty-five, and who, more than anyone else, has taught me that the well-exercised human body, well beyond youth, is capable of feats that very few realize. Peter modeled the calisthenics and stretch exercises depicted in chapter thirteen and is a veteran

9

squash champion. He also is the culprit who got me to join him in marathon training!

I have learned much about physical fitness in general, and also the basic fundamentals of my two personally most-frequented games, from both teachers and playing partners alike. In squash I thank my teachers Khalid Mir and Rick Rescigno, and my aggressive opponents John Leathers, Kevan Pickens, and Warren Young, who rarely have let me win, and who thereby have forced me to face and deal with the reality of my limitations. In golf I am indebted to professionals Harry Cooper and Ed Nicholson, and to my frequent partners, who regularly humble me and teach me, thereby, a lot about myself: Ames Brown, Mike Hilton, John Reese, and John Sturman.

This book has been enhanced by the cartoons of another squash friend, Mike Witte, and by the stretch and exercise line drawings of Peter Harrison.

I am especially indebted to friends who helped me by giving me much constructive advice in the development of this book: Doctor Charles Carr (who took the jogging photographs) and Reverend Jimmy DiRaddo, my associates at the Christian Counselling and Psychotherapy Center; George O'Carroll, graduate of Gordon-Conwell Seminary; Allison Brown, my former secretary, now herself in seminary training; Sharon Behrens, her successor, my present dedicated and totally indispensable office helpmeet; and fellow parishioners Joanna Farquharson, who suggested the opening chapter title "Fit for the King," Mary Hays, and Pamela Klein. Special thanks are also due to Roseann Isgro, who not only advised on many very helpful improvements, but also typed almost the entire manuscript.

Finally I give my loving and appreciative thanks to LouAnn, my wife, who not only patiently tolerated my papers all over the dining-room table as I wrote, but also sacrificially put up with the temporary general disruption of family togetherness; and to Jennifer (age seven) and Justyn (age five), who gave me the frequent pleasurable distractions and relaxation that I needed regularly.

Preface

THIS BOOK IS WRITTEN with committed Christian men and women primarily in mind. Though commendably concerned preeminently with Christ and their relationship with Him, such believers are usually either woefully ignorant or culpably negligent of their responsibilities to their own physical bodies. For them, the ideas presented herein are intended to challenge, to shake from complacency, and to inspire to responsible self-protective action. Those reading this who are not concerned with the religious aspect of our human experience might nevertheless find in this book a useful summary of many of the physiological principles of bodily well-being.

God gave to every man and woman a body to live in for the very limited period in which we exist physically in space and time. He expects every one of us to take proper care of this GI (general issue): to protect it; to feed it well, but not too well; to give it the exercise it needs regularly and enthusiastically; and to keep it in good shape spiritually, psychologically, and physically.

Physical well-being is the message of this book, to Christian and non-Christian alike. Although the chapters can be read in any order and still be understood, there is an intended sequence. However I personally regard the last three chapters as the vital message I really want to share. I make no claim to being a prophet, but God can many times choose to use human means to reveal His will to His children. I believe it is His will for all Christians to be physically in excellent shape and to develop

11

and maintain protective and preventative attitudes with regard to injury or illness. To this end this book should contribute a little.

As you go through these pages, however superficially, please do not fail to turn to the many appendixes at the end when you come to the places where they are referred to. They are not just of academic interest, but significantly help one's intelligent understanding of the main text.

My prayer is that all who read these chapters may appreciate more deeply our solemn responsibility and obligation to God to achieve and maintain complete health in our bodies as well as in our minds and spirits.

1

Fit for the King

HAVING SPOKEN many times before a wide variety of Christian gatherings, I have found that any mention of the evils of smoking, drinking, drug abuse, or extramarital sex can be guaranteed to elicit a response of enthusiastic agreement. But if I bring up such topics as diet, weight control, or the need for a regular vigorous-exercise program, I can see and feel the resistance in the audience. At one such meeting, a woman told me afterwards that I had not been spiritual enough—that I had made some of the saints feel very uncomfortable!

There seems little interest in the subject of bodily well-being or physical fitness, with very rare exceptions, among those in positions of leadership in the church. Preoccupation with spirituality can become a smoke screen preventing a good honest look at one's poor physical shape. In terms of the "whole man" concept, Christians can be just as guilty as pagans (who neglect the spirit) in their own neglect of the body.

As a Christian, a physician, and an amateur athlete (of more enthusiasm than ability), I have for many years been concerned about the low view of the human body expressed by many evangelical Christians, who have regarded it merely as a temporary burden instead of the temple of the Holy Spirit. As a result, many Christians have failed to give their bodies the protective and nutritive care that they need. They often pamper their bodies with expensive clothing, jewelry, cosmetics, hair styling, and so forth because they want to look good on the outside. But they're sick on the inside, because they lack discipline and an appropriate biblical value system. Speaking to women, but equally applicable to men, Paul said that they should ". . . adorn themselves in modest apparel, with shamefacedness and sobriety; not with broided hair, or gold, or pearls, or costly array; But . . . with good works" (1 Timothy 2:9, 10).

Being often more concerned with outward appearances, many Christians have let themselves degenerate more rapidly than they otherwise would, through the neglect of becoming unfit because of grossly inadequate physical exercise. I am convinced that keeping physically fit and healthy is one of the Christian believer's most vital responsibilities, yet one that is frequently ignored.

There are lots of books on spiritual fitness in religious bookstores, and there are lots of books on physical fitness in secular bookstores, but I've never seen a book written specifically for Christians, exhorting them to take care of their God-given physical bodies. It is my purpose to show that keeping healthy and physically fit *is* a Christian responsibility. When this aspect of life is neglected, our development into whole men and women reflecting the personality of Jesus Christ is severely stunted.

I think this book is unique. Every author thinks his book is, of course; but I feel that this one presents a rare kind of challenge to believers, and that it is biblical. It strives first to make us feel guilty for our self-neglect but then also to inspire us to catch a glimpse of how much better our lives could be when we daily experience and radiate vitality and physical health.

Christian, this book is unorthodox, radical, and even subversive. It is threatening to the complacent. It could significantly change your daily routine. Its ideas

changed mine. But if you are satisfied with your life-
style and don't see that God might have anything new to
reveal to you, close this book quickly and return rapidly
to the security of your familiar way.

Perhaps, however, you are a little curious, "What's
new now?" you ask. "What's all this about fitness?
What's in it for me to be physically fit? Isn't being filled
with the Spirit of God the ultimate experience in life?
Isn't Jesus all you need?"

Yes, Jesus *is* all you need: But are *you* all Jesus needs?

Could you, for example, be a more effective servant of
Christ if your body and mind were in better shape?
Wouldn't you do a better job of carrying out God's will
for your life if your physical and mental capacities were
usable by God to their maximum potential? Most Christians would agree that training and disciplining the mind
and the zealous development of their spiritual lives are
essential in their becoming effective servants of God in
our complex society. It is only logical that the physical
body is not exempt from the same demands.

There are many Christians who are much more devout
and spiritual than I ever knew how to be. But many of
them are miserable or even neurotic. They seem to have
so many problems—emotional or physical. They're
sound in doctrine, but there's no joy in their lives. It
cannot be just a coincidence that many of them are
overweight, underexercised, or both. I am absolutely
certain that for most Christians there is a direct relationship between physical well-being and enthusiastic ef-
fectiveness in witness to the Lord.

Think about this: If, right now, starting this week, you
began a slowly progressive, nonpainful, diet and exercise program, here's what would happen: You'd start to
feel better; you'd function better; you'd relate to others
better; you'd serve the Lord better; you'd not only enjoy
a renewed zest for life, but you'd also retain or return to

good or even excellent health; and, incidentally, you'd probably live longer.

I am concerned in this book with that which I know from both personal and professional experience to be the greatest area of neglect in our evangelical Christian community—the matter of taking good care of all the needs of our God-given bodies—bodies in which God the Holy Spirit has chosen to dwell.

In his first letter to the Christians in Corinth, the apostle Paul wrote: "What? know ye not that your body is the temple of the Holy Ghost which is in you, which ye have of God, and ye are not your own? For ye are bought with a price: therefore glorify God in your body, and in your spirit, which are God's" (1 Corinthians 6:19, 20). Consider also his admonition to the believers in Rome: "I beseech you therefore, brethren, by the mercies of God, that ye present your bodies a living sacrifice, holy, acceptable unto God, which is your reasonable service" (Romans 12:1).

This book is concerned, not with faith healing or medical treatment, but with prevention. Take care of your body *before* it gets sick. Get into great physical shape and enjoy the euphoria of serving and praising the Lord, with a healthy spirit, mind, and body. Get fit for the King.

2

Your Body—
Temple or Ruin?

LET'S START by doing a quick self-evaluation. How are you feeling today? Tired, yawning, sleepy in the afternoon, drowsy after a heavy meal, listless, fatigued, depressed in mood? Are you anxious, irritable, impatient, uptight, hostile, worried, fearful? Any indigestion? Too much or too little appetite? Nausea, constipation, or diarrhea? Poor interpersonal relationships? Problems with authority or fulfilling responsibilities? Sleep poorly last night? Are you more than ten pounds overweight? Flight of stairs, short run for a bus make you breathless? Mowing the lawn, raking the leaves, shoveling the snow almost lead to collapse? Losing interest in your job, work around the house, the kids, social or church activities? Not as zealous in worship of God as you used to be? Less interested in sex (granted your age) than you used to be? Or less able to perform? Too tired? Too tired! (I'll be saying more about this in a later chapter.)

Mark Twain once said, "Whenever I feel the urge to take some exercise, I sit down until the urge passes off"!

We have our superathletes, of course, who can compete successfully with the best in the world in the Olympics and other international competitive events. But the average American takes little exercise after leaving high school, and even less after college. We begin to realize in our thirties and forties how overweight and unfit we have become. But the process began in the late teens and early twenties, once we were no longer in school. A life-style of maintenance physical conditioning

18

must become a high-value-oriented activity and be begun, on an individual basis if necessary, as soon as the organized games and sports of youth are left behind.

In Europe there are thousands of amateur clubs and teams that men and women can join to remain participant, and competitive, if they desire, on into late middle life, and even beyond. Soccer, rugby, cricket, field hockey, lacrosse, tennis, badminton, squash rackets, cycling, swimming, gymnastics, fell walking, track and field athletics, and cross-country-running clubs abound. Any person has a wide selection of activities with which he or she can choose to keep physically fit. Thank God for our YMCAs, health clubs, high-school tracks, and other facilities available here; but what we really need more than equipment is a change of attitude.

Recently I visited one of the finest athletic clubs in the world. It has over ten thousand members. I was told that less than two thousand of them use the many excellent athletic facilities. The rest use the club mainly for eating, drinking, or sleeping! Yes, it is our attitude toward bodily health and fitness that influences the shape we're in. The whole country needs a change of attitude through which men and women throughout life would become involved in continuing physical or sporting endeavors. We need more amateur clubs and organizations which provide participation, and fewer professional ball games, which keep most Americans sitting down just watching!

Mercifully, however, some progress is being made. Sometime ago, I saw a large notice in a doctor's waiting room, which said, A HUNDRED THOUSAND DOCTORS HAVE QUIT SMOKING. MAYBE THEY KNOW SOMETHING WE NEED TO KNOW! The medical profession is slowly beginning to put more emphasis on preventive medicine, which includes teaching the avoidance of self-destructive habits and giving more attention to a balanced diet and a physical-conditioning program.

Many elementary schools are now teaching children the effects of smoking *before* they get started. Medical students are being taught more now about prevention, and doctors are teaching their patients more about how to avoid potential medical problems.

I also wish that the clergy, who have equal if not greater influence than physicians on people's minds, would preach sermons more often exhorting the spiritually faithful to be also physically fit to the glory of God. Though preaching much about sin, they rarely give any practical, workable definition of it. Sin for me is to do, or not do, anything which could harm my body, my self-esteem, or any relationships with God or others. To be perfectly blunt, I consider that to malnourish my body with excess food or allow it to deteriorate through lack of exercise are very serious sins. Preachers should have the guts to tell their Christian listeners when they see that they are sinning in these areas. Physical fitness and true spirituality are interrelated and inseparable.

A famous high school in England, dating back to the thirteenth century, has as its motto the Latin statement, *Mens Sana in Corpore Sano.* "A healthy mind in a healthy body."

Quoting the ancient Greeks, then-President-elect John F. Kennedy in the December 26, 1960, issue of *Sports Illustrated* wrote, "Physical fitness is not only one of the most important keys to a healthy body, it is the basis of dynamic and creative intellectual activity. Intelligence and skill can only function at the peak of their capacity when the body is healthy and strong; hardy spirits and tough minds usually inhabit sound bodies."

It has been said that the advent of the automobile in America has killed more people by inactivity than by accidents. We are so often in such a hurry to get to the corner drugstore and back that our impatience leads us to jump into the car instead of enjoying and benefiting from a few minutes exercise by walking. An average of

fifty thousand people die each year in highway accidents, whereas almost a million die annually of heart
attacks. Many of these are either preventable altogether
or at least postponable in individuals whose hearts are
maintained in good shape through regular exercise.

The medical signs and symptoms of inactivity are
scary. A body that isn't used, quickly deteriorates. Astronauts have to do vigorous exercises out in space to
compensate for the ease of living in a weightless environment. If the extent of your exercise consists of walking from your car to the television set, you will eventually literally fall apart: Your lungs will become less effective in the task of oxygen and carbon-dioxide exchange;
your heart will grow less efficient; you will lose muscle
tone; your bones will become more brittle due to loss of
calcium; your blood vessels will become less pliable,
and your body will become weaker, especially in the
matter of the blood's ability to resist infection. You will
then become much more vulnerable to colds and other
upper-respiratory infections. If you suffer any injury to
bone or muscle, you will take longer to heal. Worst of all,
your mind will become affected, as evidenced by yawning and a drowsy feeling all day, slowed thought processes, a frequent sense of being "too tired" to do even
minor tasks, and eventually by failing memory and declining ability to think logically and rationally.

By contrast, consider these rewards of physical fitness:
increased zest for living, generally; increased available
energy for all daily tasks; ability to work efficiently,
without fatigue; increased sexual libido, both desire and
ability; significantly improved performance and health
of all vital organs, especially the heart, lungs, and blood
vessels; greater speed of healing of all bone and soft
tissues in case of illness or injury; greater resistance to
infections; better tolerance to emotional stress; much-
improved sleep at night, and ability to rest and relax
properly, when necessary, during the day; reduced fat

deposits and, therefore, better control of body weight; decreased pulse rate and blood pressure (signs of cardiovascular health); decreased reaction time (quicker reflexes); fewer gastrointestinal symptoms, such as indigestion or constipation; less chance of emotional depression or anxiety; general feeling of well-being, leading to attitudes of optimism, increased productivity, improved interpersonal relationships, and considerable sharpening in thought processes due to the total dependence of the cerebral cortex (conscious-mind part of the brain) on efficient heart-lung functioning. Finally, not medically proven, but the author's invariable personal experience—a much-increased desire and capacity to worship, thank, praise, and serve the Lord to the fullness of one's abilities and talents.

A healthy body is fun to have, but to be unhealthy is miserable. A healthy body is delightful, comfortable, and pleasant to look at; while an unhealthy or fat body is ugly, or even grotesque. God often permits some suffering in the Christian experience for the purpose of restoring a rebellious, or more often, a lazy or neglectful follower back into a more intimate fellowship with Himself. Some pain and discomfort, therefore, either in physical or emotional form, can happen to anyone; but much that we suffer is *not* God's will. We have brought it upon ourselves by our own neglect. Whereas God sometimes uses sickness as a loving means of bringing back a lost sheep, He is not to be held responsible for all the results of our own stupidity in not living within the limits of natural laws.

If we don't exercise sufficiently and regularly, we are highly vulnerable to a sudden, fatal heart attack. If we persist in smoking over a pack of cigarettes a day, natural law decrees that our lungs will suffer. If we drink alcohol at a higher rate than our livers can metabolize it, we know that they will eventually develop cirrhosis. If we continue to eat sugar-filled junk food in calorific excess

Bounding with joy across the miles.

of our energy expenditure, we cannot blame God if we gain weight. And let's not blame Him either if we have a tough time giving up all these self-destructive habits. We know the rules. We know the penalties for breaking them. "Cause and effect" is one of the inexorable principles of natural law in any form. Cause and effect is the first fundamental of the scientific method, and the overruling essence of general revelation in all of space and time. We ignore it at our peril.

One of the slogans of the American Health Foundation is, "Nobody takes better care of you than you." It stresses that, since many of the diseases of man as yet unconquered are in fact man-made, it follows that they are therefore preventable. But let us not think of it as being the responsibility of organized medicine or government departments of health to deliver to us the well-being we desire. True, some progress has been made in prevention, especially in the area of infectious diseases, with immunization programs. But remember that throughout history no illness or disease has ever been eliminated by curing it. Curing merely restores the individual to health. The disease survives to afflict others, until preventive methods eventually conquer it, and even then only for as long as our guards remain up.

We need, therefore, as individuals, to take upon ourselves the responsibility of practicing our own preventive medicine. The attitude of "it can't happen to me" is unrealistic, foolish, and dangerous. Yes it *can* happen to me, to you, to any one of us who ignorantly or willfully defies natural law. We live within the confines of nature as God made it, and He does not make exceptions. ". . . for he . . . sendeth rain on the just and on the unjust" (Matthew 5:45).

Let us look next at some general considerations about our physical natures, and then we'll get into the matters of the avoidance of harmful habits and the establishment of healthy ones.

3

Upholding the Temple

As a youth, I was an athlete of very modest success through high school and college, but long years of postgraduate and postdoctoral training significantly reduced my physical activity level throughout my late twenties and my thirties. By the age of thirty-seven, when I finally married (for the first and I hope only time), I stood five feet ten inches tall, and I weighed almost two hundred pounds; with loving, wifely cooking I was gradually turning into a baby whale! Something had to be done.

For me it was three things: 1. Reduction of my dietary intake; 2. running (jogging if you prefer); and 3. playing squash rackets, a four-wall court game faster than handball or racquetball, and a lot better workout than tennis. I also much enjoy playing golf, but I don't consider the five-mile walk involved as being of any significant contribution to my exercise program. The pace is too slow. For you, in addition to controlled eating, it could be any one or two of a number of activities.

These points, however, are important: Whatever you choose as your health-giving, weight-controlling exercise, it must be: 1. Something that you could learn to enjoy sufficiently for you to be willing to do it thoroughly and regularly (a minimum of three times weekly); 2. something that produces sufficient calorific expenditure first to reduce and then to control your body weight; and 3. something that results in sufficient oxygen consump-

A quick-moving squash game is fun and healthy.

tion to produce a training effect which would promote fitness in these essential organs—the heart, blood vessels, and the lungs.

All these requirements could be fulfilled very adequately by simple brisk walking, preferably progressing to jogging short distances, and ultimately to running at a good pace for longer distances. Walking and running have the added advantages of being easy to do, they are usually the most convenient, the least expensive, the least demanding of equipment and facilities, and by far the most efficient in terms of calories and oxygen used up in the time available. (*See* chapter 14 for more on this.)

It is not enough, however, for me simply to state dogmatically that all Christians should diet and exercise. This is indeed the message of this book, but ideas and principles need to be explained, illustrated, and repeated again and again for them to be received, believed, and acted upon. My missionary zeal, therefore, is to share with others something great that I have discovered, in order that they may benefit also. Becoming physically fit has transformed my life: I feel so healthy every day, and this has led to immeasurable improvement in functioning in all areas.

Many of the patients I see daily in my psychiatric practice would never have needed to come if they had been in excellent physical condition. Obviously not all, but I am certain that many of the men and women who go to their family physicians or pastors, and via them to a psychiatrist or marital counselor, complain of a multitude of minor problems which often might not have arisen if all members of the family had been diet and weight conscious and had been in a regular exercise or conditioning program.

I have, furthermore, found that the pursuit of a good nutritional and activity routine by patients seeing me for a wide variety of minor neurotic problems has led to many quite dramatic improvements without the use of medications or protracted in-depth psychotherapy. In many instances, a mildly depressive mood has been elevated, moderate anxiety attacks partially alleviated, poor self-image problems improved by an increased sense of identity and ego strength, and marital and family conflicts often helped to be reduced or even to disappear through the development of new, shared activities and better communication arising out of great feelings of physical well-being.

This sounds as if it were some kind of magic, or at least too good to be true. Of course, not all emotional or interpersonal-relationship problems can be cured by simply dieting and jogging! Obviously, also, merely getting the body into first-class shape doesn't automatically cure problems of the mind or emotions. Certainly serious psychiatric disorders still need psychiatric treatment, and the underlying causes of many neuroses and personality problems still need to be discovered, understood, and either accepted or changed where possible. However, this much is certainly true: A life-style that has respect for bodily well-being, by careful attention both to what is put into the system and also to the physical effort put out by it, leads to a significant reduction of aggravating symptoms, both subjectively and with respect to relating to others. This is a good biological example of the cause-and-effect principle.

If you are an atheist, agnostic, or purely a nominal Christian, my first concern for you is that you should find Christ as your personal Saviour. To come to accept and then to know Jesus as Lord in your life is not only the most important decision you could ever make here on earth, but it also represents a choice which will affect your eternal destiny.

This book, however, is written for Christians like you who have already taken that step; your life has already been changed dramatically. After years of living the fleshly, "natural" life, striving only to satisfy physical and material wants, you have now become a person striving to respond to the Spirit rather than the flesh. If Jesus is your Lord, what more could you possibly need? Read on.

Well, praise the Lord, I'm with you in your spiritual experiences. I also have been born again and Spirit filled, and the God-shaped void within me has been replaced fully by our indwelling Saviour.

So now I have toward you all a different kind of missionary zeal, having become satisfied with your spiritual security. As Christians in fellowship together in Him, we are obligated to help each other progress in our pilgrimage through life, to mature as colaborers and servants of Christ, and to share all things which are edifying to our growth. For this cause also do I desire to share with you that which God has first revealed to me. (Forgive me if I sound like the apostle Paul! As judged by his impact on human history, next to Christ Himself, Paul was the greatest man who ever lived.)

To my own great surprise, after years of painfully slow spiritual growth, God has led me back to an appreciation of the physical side of my nature. This is not, mercifully, a regression to former lusts, but a progression to a fresh realization of the triunity of man: The inseparable nature of the physical, psychological, and spiritual elements within us all, not one of which must be neglected for the supposed sake of the other two.

Born again as a relatively young man, a medical student at the time, I was already experienced in this world enough to have enjoyed many of its pleasures. And I'm not going to be superspiritual and claim, as one hears in so many testimonies, that they did not satisfy. No, the truth is that they *did* satisfy. I *thoroughly* enjoyed them and still would today if those pleasures were all I desired.

But they are not all I desire now; and they were not

even then, as I soon discovered through two things that
happened. First, I found that the pleasures didn't last. As
their novelty passed, their stimulus also faded. As actions led to habits, they became commonplace—their
excitements and fulfillments waned and dimmed. Second, I found something better. I found Christ; or, rather,
He found me and in finding me offered me life on a
different plane, life more thoroughly fulfilling, life in the
spiritual dimension.

I, therefore, rejoiced in the life of the Spirit and re-
jected the life of the flesh, but I overreacted. Perhaps
somewhat expectedly, in my immaturity, my religious-
conversion experience resulted in an aversion to anything physical, a repulsion from the flesh and the body. I
felt the way Paul expressed so powerfully in his letter to
the Christians in Rome: "O wretched man that I am! who
shall deliver me from the body of this death?" (Romans
7:24). I deprecated my imperfect body, bound to this
world, with all its physical needs, cravings, desires, and
uncontrollable temptations, and longed for the resur-
rected body, in the hereafter, which has no sin. I thought
of Paul's comment to the Philippians: "He [Jesus] will
transfigure the body belonging to our humble state, and
give it a form like that of his own resplendent body, by
the very power which enables him to make all things
subject to himself" (Philippians 3:21 NEB).

Yet, then, as I progressed through medical school, my
appreciation of the structure and workings of the human
body excited me. Learning and discovering about this
amazing miracle filled me with profound awe at the
progressive acts of God, which resulted in this magnificent creation. Human anatomy and physiology taught
me how our bodies work normally. Then the study of
pathology sobered me to understand how it can work
abnormally; how from a point of perfection, in youth, it
slowly but inexorably degenerates to the point where it
eventually yields up the soul and spirit for their return

to God, whence they came.

I learned about diseases that can cause premature death, but I also learned that premature death and an awful lot of pain and discomfort which come during life are often the direct results of man's self-destructiveness and neglect.

What destructiveness and neglect?

Inadequate or excessive nutrition is the self-destructiveness, and lack of physical exercise is the neglect. These are some of the sins you and I need to avoid.

"I can't stand the physical," complained a staff nurse with whom I once worked. "Most people are so concerned about their carnal bodies that they neglect their souls and spirits." She was a devout, believing Christian, and she had a point, of course. Many people, including some professing Christians, do ignore their spiritual needs and pursue happiness and satisfaction mainly through possessions or activities of a material or physical nature.

As Christians, it is appropriate that we should be concerned to live our lives in the spirit rather than the flesh. "For to be carnally minded is death; but to be spiritually minded is life and peace . . . . For if ye live after the flesh, ye shall die: but if ye through the Spirit do mortify the deeds of the body, ye shall live" (Romans 8:6, 13). The words *soma* and *sarx* in the New Testament Greek usually translated "body" and "flesh," respectively, are not synonymous. *Body* means the physical temple, a creation of God, not in itself implicated in moral issues. *Flesh,* by contrast, does have a moral connotation. It is used in the description of those thoughts and activities of the body which are contrary to the influence of the Spirit of God within it. We have, therefore, a responsibility to take care of the body (*soma*), to keep it healthy, and to use it in accordance with God's will, led by the Spirit, resisting the flesh (*sarx*).

On this basis, the nurse betrayed some serious inconncies. Though in practicing her religion she did not smoke or drink any alcohol (commendable avoidances), she was nevertheless grossly overweight and admitted that she never exercised. She was just as "physical" as others whom she accused of indulging in the "lusts of the flesh." She couldn't resist the physical pleasure of eating to excess and preferred the physical comfort of a deep armchair to the health-giving stimulus of a brisk walk.

She also had too low a view of the physical body. She seemed oblivious to the fact that her own body, which she was slowly destroying through neglect and mistreatment, was something very special, uniquely fashioned by God.

The human frame is the most complicated and magnificent structure in the known universe. The smooth, coordinated movements of our muscles and joints make the most intricate piece of machinery look clumsy, and the human brain far surpasses in abilities those of all lower animals or of the most sophisticated of computers.

Some have apparently reasonably suggested the possibility of life on other planets—if not in our own solar system, surely in others in our Milky Way galaxy. If God in His sovereignty has chosen to create intelligent life in other parts of the universe, man's eyes will never see it in the body unless He permits other created beings to visit us. As far as our own exploratory fantasies are concerned, we are forever cut off by unimaginably vast distances. A round trip, as astronauts traveling at any speed predictably attainable, would take too long. To the nearest star, Proxima Centauri, a mere four and a quarter light-years away, even a one-way trip would take far longer than a human life span.

The most we could ever hope for would be some form of interstellar or intergalactic communication, via some yet-to-be-discovered electromagnetic radiations. Even from the nearest possible other solar system, a potential reply to any message would be almost nine years in coming, and 99.9 percent of the universe is so far away that even radio messages would take thousands or even millions of years to reach their destination. God in His wisdom has chosen to isolate us on this beautiful, lonely planet. For the present time, therefore, not denying any possible future discoveries, let us respect the human body as the highest creative act of God so far revealed to us.

This body, however, does not exist just for its own sake. It is a temporary abiding place, or home, for the human soul and spirit within it and represents their outward physical manifestation in time and space. Your body and mind, therefore, and mine also, are like ambassadors appearing on earth, temporarily representing the image of God to this part of His physical creation.

Your soul, the real you, the image of God, has been given your physical body as a priceless gift. Your body is God's special creation, possessing conscious awareness, given for the purpose and privilege of serving Him in time on earth. As with every privilege, there is an accompanying responsibility—that of taking care of the gift and using it properly. *Taking care of* means respecting the natural laws affecting the body by remaining within the confines of those laws. *Properly* means in accordance with the purposes of the Creator, "God's will" for your life, which is revealed and explained through both special and general revelation.

Special revelation is God's unique message to mankind, His created beings, and is manifested through the Old and New Testament Scriptures. These portray first the teaching of the concept of monotheism; the history and law of the Israelites (God's chosen people); the instructions, warnings, poetry, and predictions of their prophets and kings; the preeminent incarnation and Resurrection of Jesus, the Christ, God in human form; and the establishment of the present, living church by the love, wisdom, and power of the Holy Spirit.

General revelation is God's message to us, manifested through the physical creation in time and space, through all natural laws, and through much of human wisdom and experience in history. All true discoveries of all the branches of science, from astronomy, through mathematics and medicine, to zoology, are examples of general revelation. They are like thinking God's thoughts after Him. Many creations of the human mind in art, music, poetry, literature, architecture, and in philosophy, and even abstract thought, are gifts revealing some of God's infinite riches, displayed by human expression and endeavor. Conversely, of course, much of human "wisdom" is at enmity with God.

We have to be discerning. None of general revelation which is genuinely from God is in conflict with His special revelation, the Scriptures, whereas some of the "wisdom" of fallen man might be. ". . . the foolishness of God is wiser than men . . . . But God hath chosen the foolish things of the world to confound the wise . . ." (1 Corinthians 1:25, 27). Christians, therefore, should at all times test what they do and don't do by the standards of Holy Writ. Scripture, correctly understood, is the overruling guideline for all human decisions and actions within the Christian belief system. The Bible is our handbook for life.

Read again the three important verses quoted at the end of Chapter 1: 1 Corinthians 6:19, 20 and Romans 12:1. These stress that it is part of God's special revelation to us that we are held responsible for keeping our bodies and minds in good physical shape and free from carnal sin. How to do this is part of general revelation, and some of what has been revealed to us occupies the remainder of this book.

4

Protecting the Temple

SINCE WE HAVE AGREED from the first three chapters that it is more fun to have a healthy than an unhealthy body, we need now to consider a few thoughts on how to protect it. A thorough general physical examination, as recommended annually past age thirty-five, will enable us both to detect any potential problem areas and also will give us the added protection of more time to treat any discovered pathology before it can become dangerous. We need now to think about some of the harmful things that we must avoid and also some of the beneficial things we can do to keep our bodies in good shape. The first of these is the subject of the next several chapters.

David said, ". . . I am fearfully and wonderfully made . . ." (Psalms 139:14). With very rare exceptions, we are all born with healthy bodies capable of living to more than a hundred years, if we would only obey all the natural laws and common-sense practices that God has revealed to us for our discipline. Want to know how? Here is a package deal for you:

1. *Meals*—three small or moderate-sized nutritional meals a day, with no in-between snacks or junk food
2. *Weight*—within ten pounds of standard for height (*see* Appendix B for weight chart)
3. *Smoking*—no smoking, unprescribed drugs, or liquor
4. *Accidents*—an accident-preventive life-style
5. *Sleep*—seven or eight hours of sleep every night, and regular, alternating periods of activity and relaxation during the day

6. *Physical examination*—an annual physical check-up
7. *Pollution*—avoidance of pollution in all its forms
8. *Exercise*—regular, brisk exercise four or five days every week

A study in California recently completed on seven thousand people evaluated a "life package" similar to this. The statistics bear out that people who follow six or seven of these principles live an average of ten years longer than those who only follow three or less. Does a whole extra decade of life appeal to you? The price is not excessive—you might even enjoy paying it!

Studies, made by experts on old age on the well-known Russian centenarians from the Ukraine and Caucasus and other long-lived people in isolated areas of northern India and western South America, have revealed many common factors in their lives. Apparently contributing to their longevity are such factors as a predominantly outdoor life-style, regular, daily, moderate exercise, diets of fruit, vegetables, and cereals raised locally and eaten fresh, low levels of emotional stress and competitiveness, and a partial or total absence of highly refined sugar foods, red meat, tobacco, environmental pollution, and hard liquor.

Not all of these factors are easily attainable by us, who live in a modern urban or suburban environment, and who are subjected to the rat-race pressures of professional and social strivings, eating mainly packaged and processed supermarket-style foods, and brought up to use wheels rather than feet for transportation. Yet, we do have some measure of control over our internal biochemical systems and our external influences and stimuli. Let us think about a few obvious life-threatening habits we all should consider soberly. First a few acute or sudden-death type situations, and then some more chronic habits, which, though taking longer to kill, are just as dangerous or destructive in the long run.

Ask yourself a few questions. Only a few of these will apply to you personally, yet all are statistically significant over the whole population. Think about these issues: Do you drive strictly at fifty-five miles per hour or less? If you transgress the law of the land, don't kid yourself that God will protect you on the road. Do you always use a seat belt with a combined shoulder harness? Are your young children secured in special, protective car seats? Try walking into a wall nose first at three miles per hour. Uncomfortable? Imagine hitting a windshield at forty or sixty miles per hour! That could be quite influential on your facial beauty, assuming, of course, that you survive the associated irreversible brain damage. I predict that air bags and crash helmets will be in common use ten years hence, also that cars will be safer then and roads less hazardous. But we need to be cautious *now*.

What about alcoholic drinks? Do you have one for the road? Or two perhaps? If so, better be humble and let your sober spouse or friend drive you home. No way does God obligate Himself to take care of you if you flagrantly transgress the natural law that drinking and driving don't mix. Remember that fifty percent of road traffic deaths, or twenty-five thousand people killed per year, are alcohol related.

Think about other safety precautions. Do you *really* know how to handle that boat or motorcycle before you set off on a short joyride? Both power boats and sailboats have their rules and regulations. We must know and abide by them if we want to enjoy the open water without jeopardizing ourselves or others. On motorized minibikes in Bermuda it is compulsory both to wear a crash helmet and to keep speed to twenty miles per hour. Narrow roads there, true, but the same principles are valid here, even if we can go a bit faster when road conditions are safe.

What about dangerous substances or equipment in the house? Do you keep all drugs and medications and all poisonous cleaning fluids out of the reach of small children? Do you have faulty wiring, leaking gas, or defective heating apparatus? Do you possess electrical appliances, power tools, high ladders, or, worst of all, firearms? We must be certain that all our items of household equipment are working properly and safely, and that they are stored carefully away from those who don't know how to use them. There are pamphlets available on home-safety tips. Try to get one, keep it in the kitchen, and encourage all family members to study it.

Also, registered or licensed or not, who needs that hand gun or rifle? A significant percentage of accidental, uncontrollable, or even premeditated homicides every year would never have occurred if there hadn't happened to have been a gun in the house. If it's there, there's always that rare but potentially fatal impulsive urge to use it when provoked. The rare chance of your needing it to catch a burglar is far less likely to happen than the violent flaring of temper in a family argument. Ever mad at your teenager, husband, wife, father, brother, or mother-in-law? If so, better get rid of that gun. One of them might use it on you!

Play golf in the rain? No problem just getting wet, in fact, it's sometimes quite exhilarating, if you're not too worried about your higher scores. But what about lightning? Imagine: You're walking off the seventeenth green; you have a stroke on the last hole, and all you need is a half to win your match. Suddenly, black overcast, deep rumblings, and bright flashes draw rapidly nearer. What to do? An agony of decision. You want to finish, but cool reason must remind you that a golfer on an open fairway with a metal club at the top of his backswing is a perfect lightning conductor. Being struck by lightning is a very quick way to go, but it's better to quit. At least you'll be around to play the next weekend.

Let's think now about less dramatic, but still potentially lethal hazards. For example, what kinds of pollution should be avoided in taking care of the body and its health needs?

Air pollution kills. The great London "pea-souper" fog of 1952 killed hundreds of elderly people with emphysema or bronchitis. Modern U.S. cities, in spite of antipollution legislation, are still unhealthy to live in. Both chemical and particulate contaminants pervade city air, which is assaulted by industrial, domestic, automobile, and aircraft wastes and exhausts. If you both live and work in the industrial area of a big city, the damage to your lungs over several years is the equivalent of that caused by smoking twenty or more cigarettes daily. Try to avoid the smoking areas of planes, buses, and trains. Secondhand smoke is just as harmful as inhaling it firsthand! If you're inflicted with chain smokers where you work, try to get close to an open window or door. Would wearing a smog mask shame them into quitting? Try to get out of the city at least once a week for a good, long walk, taking many full, deep breaths on the way, to open up the remotest air sacs in your lungs. Fresh air and brisk exercise also do wonders for sagging spirits.

Water pollution is not much of a problem now in industrialized countries, but beware of your vacation trip abroad. Montezuma's Revenge is the acute gastroenteritis you might get from local water in Mexico or other semitropical or equatorial climes. When I'm in such places, I prefer bottled or canned beverages—without ice, of course, which is made from the local water.

Noise pollution is increasingly being recognized as injurious to health. Aircraft engines oppress thousands of people only a few hundred feet below their climb corridors or glide paths on landing. Not only the Concorde SST, but all jets, must eventually be legally required to reduce their noise levels. More commonly, city living produces many other forms of noise stress: fire, police, and ambulance sirens, compressed-air drills, motors and engines of various sorts used by construction or repair crews, trucks, motorcycles, buses, and subways. Try to avoid restaurants, lounges, dance halls, or concerts where you might be insulted with amplified electric guitars and their ilk. They produce a noise level in excess of 110 decibels, which not only prevents intelligent conversation but has been proved to be irreversibly damaging to one's hearing. Included in the definition of the word *music* is the concept of a pleasurable sensation and joyous experience. By this standard, a hard-rock group spews out not creatively inspired music, but manufactured nocuous clamor.

Sunshine in excess is dangerous. Too much can lead to dehydration, second-degree burns, headaches, heatstroke, cancer of the skin, and who knows what else from all its different kinds of radiation. Ten minutes exposure at a time is enough, then take a break in the shade. If you are unable to avoid longer periods in direct sunlight, be sure to wear a wide-brimmed hat, long sleeves, and expose as little beyond your face and hands as possible.

Some plastic packages and cooking utensils can contaminate food. Glazed pottery, paints, and plaster can cause lead poisoning. Pyrex glass, stainless steel, and enamelware are safe, but copper and aluminum utensils can add their respective metals to cooked food. As budget permits, try gradually to replace these. We're advised to avoid irradiated foods, allergy-producing synthetic clothes and carpeting, hair cosmetics, insect sprays, oral contraceptives, enzyme detergents, oil and gas furnaces, microwave ovens, fluorescent lighting, and instant-on color TV! Don't ask me what's wrong with all these things! I've merely seen them mentioned in various lists of potentially dangerous items. Check your home safety guide, read all instructional booklets carefully, and don't be reserved about asking your retailer for information.

We could all become very neurotic reading about common hazards of daily living. But relax, the life of faith dictates this principle: If you know it's harmful, avoid it. (That's living under natural law, remember?) If you don't know, try to find out; but trust the Lord at the same time! He is more concerned for your well-being than you are for yourself. Your times are in His hands, and you will not die one second sooner or later than the moment He will be ready for you. If you believe this, you can live at peace and say with Job: "Though he slay me, yet will I trust in him . . ." (Job 13:15).

Now, finally, what about the overuse or misuse of medications, self- or physician prescribed? Pain killers such as aspirin and phenacetin are grossly overused. Millions of people pop pills when they are not really needed. (In a recent year on the *average*, each American consumed 280 aspirins, according to a U.S. Tariff Commission figure.) Tranquilizers, stimulants, antibiotics, laxatives, vitamins, tonics, antiseptics, and sedatives for sleep are all known to be gulped in excess of need. Usually most are initially prescribed by one's family doctor, but then the order is often automatically renewed by the friendly neighborhood pharmacist. Once the habit is developed, it becomes harder and harder to break it, and both physician and pharmacist are pressured or manipulated to keep the supply coming, neither of them wanting to lose a patient or customer. They know that many patients simply go from one doctor to another to get what they want, and that some patients' esteem of their doctor is proportional to the prescriptions he hands them.

It is a widely held false belief that for every pain and discomfort there is a curative tablet or capsule which the doctor can easily give. In fact, however, many minor symptoms require for their relief not the complication of ingesting some foreign chemical in pill form, but adequate rest, sleep, balanced diet, reasonably unstressed routine, and daily moderate exercise.

A headache, for example, is often a signal for needed

relaxation and stress reduction. Reducing the pain in the head with aspirins without reducing the tension that caused it only aggravates the problem in the long run. Taking coffee for tiredness, or a tranquilizer when feeling nervous or tense, is counterproductive if they serve only to blunt natural curative defenses or protective actions. The origin of the problems must be recognized and dealt with properly if any lasting relief is desired. Use of drugs in any form should be a last, not a first, resort.

How about illegal drugs, or legal drugs taken without prescription from a physician or in excess? Heroin is legal in England (hence there is much less drug-related crime there, incidentally), and I used to prescribe it in hospitals for such conditions as chronic, severe pain in terminal cancer. During my first week in this country, I prescribed it as a hospital resident, in all innocence, and nearly lost my job!

Very few of you reading this have ever been personally involved with "hard" drugs such as heroin, cocaine, or peyote, or hallucinogens such as LSD, STP, or DMT. More likely you have experienced a stimulant such as one of the amphetamines or Ritalin or a heavy sedative such as one of the barbiturates. All these drugs can lead to serious self-destructive habits, or even addiction in some cases. Be aware of their potential harm to yourself or loved ones, and if any become involved in excessive drug use, seek professional help quickly. There is plenty of nontechnical literature now available in good bookstores on recognizing and dealing with drug-abuse problems.

There are, however, three drugs that many people (including some Christians) often consume, and therefore must be confronted, since they are significantly harmful to our health. They are marijuana, alcohol, and nicotine, and they are each summarily indicted in the following three chapters.

5

Lure
of the Perilous Grass

FOR MANY YEARS I had thought that marijuana should
be legalized, because I had believed it to be not physically harmful or addicting. I know now that it can be very
harmful, but I still think that if *all* drugs were legalized,
as they are in the United Kingdom, it could be a means of
reducing crime. This is, of course, a highly controversial
issue, many believing that the British system would not
work over here. However, having worked for five years
as a physician in the British National Health Service, I
personally think that, with a few modifications, a similar
system could be successfully used in the U.S.A.

Addicts would be treated free by doctors and nurses,
as they are in London. They would receive known and,
therefore, controlled doses under sterile conditions,
thereby avoiding both the dangers of overdose and infection. Administration would be preferably by injection in
a special outpatient clinic to obviate the possibility of
illegal sale of hoarded pills. Treatment would be
achieved by very gradually reducing the dose, eventually to zero, over a sufficiently long period of time to
allow the body's chemistry to readjust to normal.

Pushers would lose the incentive to perpetuate the
habit in others, because if treatment were free, no one
would want to pay for what they could get for nothing. As

43

an immediate result, the mugging and burglary rate by
those desperate to buy more drugs would drop significantly. However, change seems unlikely soon. Resistance to it is generally not medical, but political.

I have, however, changed my mind about the
harmlessness of "pot," as new evidence has recently
come to light. Let us consider a brief summary of our
present understanding of drug abuse in general and
marijuana in particular.

Many young people today are experience seekers, and
taking drugs with others (peer identification) provides
them with a community experience. Some are looking
for a personality change; feeling inadequate and dis-
satisfied, they hope drugs will give them more self-
confidence and status. Others use drugs to escape emotional pain by "dropping out" or entering temporary,
blissful oblivion. For example: The psychotic may use
drugs to escape depression and suppress painful
symptoms such as delusions, hallucinations, and other
nonreality thoughts or feelings; the neurotic indulges in
order to relieve tension, stress, or anxiety, or to elevate
low mood; and the psychopath (personality disorder)
craves the thrill of the euphoria he gets when he "turns
on," or seeks to alleviate social or sexual problems.

Why do young people take drugs? Here are some possible answers:

1. They see their parents smoking and drinking and
   grow up with the attitude that drug use is socially
   acceptable behavior.
2. Peer-group pressure is a major factor. A young person with even slight feelings of inferiority or inse-
   curity finds greater acceptance in his group if he
   joins them in a pot party.
3. Simple curiosity can lead to the desire to try it "just
   once," but the pleasure derived from the relaxation,

seemingly heightened sensibility, uninhibited emotional (and sexual) expression, and group acceptance can lead to frequency of practice.

4. The risk of being caught and the fear of coming to any physical harm seem less when involved with a group of friends.

5. Drug use is often seen by youth as a symbol of independence from adult authority figures. Precisely because it is illegal, smoking pot gives expression to the normal adolescent rebellious phase. Even though he knows deep down that he still needs support, guidance, and instruction from parents and teachers, the impatient adolescent finds in this form of self-assertion a boost to his desired sense of maturity and independence.

6. Escape from an unhappy home situation, peer-group rejection, loss of a friend, parent, or sibling, financial difficulties, boyfriend or girl friend conflicts or misunderstandings, broken love affairs, or social or academic failure can sometimes be temporarily alleviated by withdrawal into drug use. Unhappily, the reality situation, however, remains unchanged and has to be faced eventually.

7. Internal problems are the most tragic causes of drug use. Low self-esteem and feelings of worthlessness, hopelessness, guilt, anxiety, or depression from whatever cause can all be temporarily escaped by taking drugs. Permanent solutions, however, remain elusive, and the dejection continues to hang like a black cloud over the sufferer, unless and until time eventually heals the wounds.

Let us now consider marijuana specifically. It is obtained from the flowers and leaves of Indian hemp, a plant with the botanical name of *Cannabis sativa*, which grows naturally in temperate climates. Its products have

been used since ancient times for intoxication or stimulation. It is not approved for medical use in either the
British or the American pharmacopoeias, and its impor-
tation into this country is illegal. It is sometimes called
grass, hash, bhang, or pot, and it is usually ingested by
inhalation like smoking a cigarette.

Let us not kid ourselves that pot smoking is confined
to youth. Many in their thirties, forties, and even fifties
are experimenting with it. Some use it to help themselves cut down on alcohol, some to revive failing sexual
powers, some use it as a tranquilizer, others to keep up
with the younger generation. All these can indeed be
achieved temporarily, but the key to recently published
findings, which should cause serious concern, is the discovery of long-range effects of use over an extended
period of time. (*See* Appendix C for references.)

Now, how can you recognize someone on pot? Consider these physical, emotional, and behavioral changes.
A person in the early stages of use will appear from time
to time to be "stoned." He may have a glazed appearance in his eyes, which may also be slightly red. He will
be animated, talkative, giggly, have uncontrollable hilar-
ity, and be apparently very happy. He tries to dominate
any conversation and seems unable to listen or to remain
quiet. He may well say things out of character for him:
He may use words of profanity, or express opinions
which are silly, unkind, untrue, hurtful, meaningless, or
hostile. He may possibly complain of thirst, hunger,
craving for sweet foods, dizziness, nausea, drowsiness,
or abdominal pain. He may well seem very confused,
apprehensive, or depressed, be inarticulate or mentally
dull. He is usually quite restless or agitated, and man-
ifests loss of reality contact by saying or doing foolish or
inappropriate things. You might think he is drunk, but
his breath does not stink of alcohol.

When not high on a recent dose, because so much

marijuana is retained in the body, other signs are manifested between trips, especially after protracted use. Experienced pot smokers suffer from distorted emotional responses, dullness and disorder of thought processes, impairment of judgment, slothfulness, lethargy, difficulty with verbalization, and a slowing down of a sense of passage of time. They manifest poor motivation, proneness to error, reduced capacity to take responsibility, memory loss, especially for important details, carelessness, and lack of attention or ability to concentrate. They usually tell lies to parents or friends to avoid admitting to their habit. This deception can only lead eventually to alienation. Those with higher intelligence or education show the greatest deterioration, usually leading to job or school failure. The user's proficiency at driving a car is impaired, even when he has not smoked pot recently, by reduced ability to gauge distance, speed, or road conditions.

The impaired judgment tragically leads to loss of control and inhibitions. This can lead to the use of more dangerous drugs, mixing the pot with alcohol, which potentiates the symptoms, or acting sexually in a manner often later regretted. Intoxication with marijuana specifically lowers sexual inhibitions and exposes the user to unhealthy sexual temptations. Interpersonal relationships invariably suffer because of easy irritability, hostility, impatience, and even the delusional thought processes of paranoia. People with poor ego strength or a borderline (potential) schizoid personality can easily be pushed over into a psychosis (serious mental disorder) by the use of marijuana. Adolescents or young adults who have not yet developed a strong sense of personal indentity are especially vulnerable to drug-induced mental or emotional breakdowns. (*See* Appendix C for a brief account of the mechanism of action of marijuana.)

Remember that our bodies and minds are the temples of God's Holy Spirit. Paul warns the Corinthians, "If any man defile the temple of God, him shall God destroy; for the temple of God is holy, which temple ye are" (1 Corinthians 3:17). In addition to incurring the wrath of God by defiling the body, there are several reasons why Christians should not partake of marijuana.

First, remember that our bodies are intended by God to be used for His purposes, and that we are to live by faith. To be fully yielded to this is impossible while under the influence of intoxicants. Our bodies cannot be effective vehicles for expressing the Spirit within if we fool around with them as if they were experimental laboratories. It is not possible to "glorify God in your body" if that body is not physically and mentally in first-class working order, and if you are not living by faith. Remember that ". . . whatsoever is not of faith is sin" (Romans 14:23).

Second, since God Himself is the ultimate reality, the Christian's personal relationship with God is his ultimate source of joy. The pot smoker is trying to escape from reality by obtaining his artificial "high." The Christian, by contrast, finds his high by relating to reality and doing God's will in the real world. Jesus is the best high. The joy of relating to Him cannot remotely be duplicated by temporary trips into euphoria, illusion, excitement, exaggerated sensations, erotic stimulation, or altered perceptions.

The oft-heard claims that marijuana heightens one's sense of reality and deepens insights are purely subjective experiences. The high mood and insights cannot be shared with others, and objective creative ability is not, in fact, increased. The experience does not lead to anything of value beyond itself. It is narcissistic pleasure for its own sake, unable to lead to any lasting measurable achievements.

On the other hand, as the Reverend Peter Moore has written,

> Hobbies, sports, good music, an exciting conversation, spirit-filled worship of God, the expression of some creative gift, the reading of a good book, the discovery of new places, the making of new friends all have value at many levels [and] they continue to have a positive effect on the individual. Sobriety is not the grim quenching of joy, but the positive engagement of one's mind [and body] for all that leads to personal wholeness.

Listen also to the apostle Peter: "Wherefore gird up the loins of your mind, be sober . . . . As obedient children, not fashioning yourselves according to the former lusts in your ignorance . . . . be ye holy in all manner of conversation" (1 Peter 1:13–15).

Third, the Christian is not at liberty to disobey the laws of the society in which he lives, even if he thinks that some of them are overly strict or that their penalties are too severe. The only possible exception to this would be situations in which civil laws are actually morally unjust or contrary to the revealed Word of God, such as the civil rights problems in this country recently, or as in past or present totalitarian regimes. Drug-abuse laws, however, are hardly in this category and, like it or not, the facts are that sale of marijuana is illegal, and God's Word clearly teaches that we are to submit to civil authority. "Let every soul be subject unto the higher powers. For there is no power but of God: the powers that be are ordained of God . . . . For rulers are not a terror to good works, but to the evil . . . . Wherefore ye must needs be subject, not only for wrath, but also for conscience sake" (Romans 13:1, 3, 5).

Finally, the Christian should heed his calling as the

"salt of the earth" and the "light of the world." Rather than being led astray by others, he should seek to lead others to experience the new life in Christ he has himself found. Smoking marijuana is learned behavior, an acquired taste. Pot smokers are lured into the habit by the enthusiasm of others. They are led astray, as Peter Laurie writes in a book on drugs ". . . by an active society of smokers who will welcome the novice and persuade him that the unpleasant sensations he first gets from the drug are in fact delightful and worth repeating." The victorious Christian, by contrast, resists such seductions and heeds the words of Paul: "And be not conformed to this world: but be ye transformed by the renewing of your mind, that ye may prove what is that good, and acceptable, and perfect, will of God" (Romans 12:2).

6

Enemy of the Brain

ALMOST TEN MILLION Americans are either outright alcoholics or "problem drinkers" whose consumption is
enough to cause serious problems both to themselves
and others. This still leaves 70 to 80 million men and
women in this country, many of them Christians, who
drink in moderation, and are rather proud of the fact that
they never get drunk. Whereas I do not share the view
that if someone partakes of alcohol, he cannot be a Christian, I nevertheless am committed to the belief that temperance is a personal quality to be aimed at by all who
profess Christ as Lord in their lives.

Although Christians differ in their opinions as to
whether or not drinking alcohol is a sin, most would
agree that the Christian virtue of self-control is required
of all of us. Although total abstention is the perfect standard, Christians who do drink are obligated to be strict
with their own self-discipline. We are in danger of losing the protective and guiding influence of the Holy
Spirit when alcohol, in clouding intellectual functioning
and loosening emotional restraint, usurps the control the
Spirit should have over us, thereby forming a barrier
between us and God.

There is no guaranteed "safe" level of drinking because individuals differ widely in their vulnerability.
Alcohol, being extremely water soluble, is rapidly absorbed through the stomach, enters the bloodstream in

seconds, and immediately is carried to the brain, a few heartbeats later. There it interferes with the release of oxygen to the brain cells, many of which die as a result. Alcohol, even in very small doses, causes blood cells to clump together, or sludge, and these can block minute capillaries, depriving local areas of the brain of vital nutrients. For reasons not yet clearly understood, some people are apparently much more sensitive than others to this highly destructive mechanism.

Remember that relaxed, woozy sensation you experience when the alcohol gets to the brain? Remember that pleasant feeling you get when it first hits you? Well, that's several hundred brain cells dying. They are permanently lost; brain cells cannot regenerate.

Even though our brains contain between 15 and 20 billion individual cells, the loss of thousands of them, with each drink, over a period of several years, eventually leads to atrophy, or actual loss of substance. This causes an undeniable loss of intellectual ability, which compounds the inevitable changes of senility in one's declining years, the very time of life when one is concerned to stay "with it" for as long as possible. Cassio said to Iago: "O God, that men should put an enemy in their mouths to steal away their brains! That we should with joy, pleasance, revel, and applause transform ourselves into beasts!" (Shakespeare's *Othello:* Act II, Scene 3.)

Alcohol is broken down in the liver to sugars which are then stored as fat, leading to undesirable weight gain, unless adequate exercise prompts further breakdown to waste products. Taken daily, even in small doses, it eventually begins to damage the liver, especially if taken on an empty stomach. Fortunately, unlike the brain, liver cells can regenerate, but only during periods of abstinence, when they are not being overwhelmed with yet more alcohol. These periods of relief are essential to recovery. It is less harmful to the liver to have a binge on a Saturday night and then abstain totally for the rest of the week, than to inflict it daily with no letup. This doesn't mean that the binge is okay. It still kills brain cells, but daily, small amounts of alcohol can cause the liver to become fatty, and, after about fifteen years of continuous abuse, it may become the victim of cirrhosis, an irreversible and potentially fatal degenerative condition.

How can you tell if a family member or friend is in danger of progressing from a social drinker to a problem drinker? When should such a one either quit completely or at the least seek professional help? Here's what to look for:

1. He/she makes stronger drinks for himself than for his guests.
2. He seems to be able to enjoy drinking alone, as much or more than if in the company of family or friends.
3. He craves his first drink of the day, and may even have it before noon. Morning drinking is an especially sinister symptom.
4. He tends to be evasive about his habit and usually divides his admitted number of drinks by two or three when stating his consumption.
5. He may slip alcohol into his orange juice or coffee or otherwise try to disguise his intake.
6. He may have had an alcohol-related traffic violation.
7. He may be unable to sleep without a stiff drink.

Two or more of these signs are strong indications that something firm must be done at once to halt an otherwise irreversible downward spiral.

Whereas I am personally convinced that alcohol is

harmful, I recognize that some Christians are less concerned. I have, therefore, a few words of caution for Christians who do not feel convinced that they ought or need to be total abstainers. By these comments I am in no way condoning the use of alcohol in any form, but rather advising of some vital principles to be remembered by those Christians who do choose to drink.

Morris Chafetz, M.D., former director of the National Institute on Alcohol Abuse and Alcoholism, has stated that one and a half ounces of pure alcohol per twenty-four hours must be regarded as the upper limit of "safe" drinking. (This is, of course, only a statistical average. For thousands of alcoholics now in Alcoholics Anonymous, and many other people, even one drop is too much.) This one and a half ounces is contained in three one-ounce shots of 100-proof liquor (which is 50% alcohol), or in twelve ounces of wine, or in thirty-two ounces of any light beer. More than this consumption will increase the concentration of alcohol in the blood to above 0.05%, at which point many brain functions begin to be adversely affected. It would take the liver at least two hours to fully metabolize the one and a half ounces, if taken all at once.

What about the types of alcohol? Within the limits of the amounts just recommended, remember one or two other relevant points. Beer, lager, ale, and stout are all very fattening, have a high calorie/low nutritional quotient, give a gassy, bloated feeling, and have the danger that, though low in alcohol percentage, they are usually drunk in large volumes. Frequently, therefore, at the end of an evening, the drinker has taken in a total of more ounces (and therefore calories) of alcohol than the slow martini sippers. Beers are *very* effective in producing weight gain, especially around the belly and hips!

Hard liquor such as whiskey, gin, vodka, rum, and

liqueurs such as brandy and sweet cordials are very high in both expense and alcohol percentage.

The high alcohol content of hard liquors relatively quickly produces in the body a biochemical imbalance. This leads to certain internal adjustment mechanisms which the system adopts in anticipation of continued supply. The victim then experiences craving, a condition in which he can only be comfortable if he indeed keeps the supply coming. This is habituation. As he persists with his habit, he needs increasing doses to produce his required level of comfort. His biochemical systems have by now progressed beyond the stage of mere adaptation. They now have to have alcohol to avoid the acute pain of withdrawal symptoms. This is addiction.

Wines, also, though containing good nutrients from grapes, are just as much of a problem as hard liquors, because of the large quantities usually consumed. Almost all of them contain as much as three times the volume of alcohol as beers, and their high sugar content significantly contributes to fat deposition.

Paul also wrote to the church at Ephesus, "And be not drunk with wine, wherein is excess; but be filled with the Spirit" (Ephesians 5:18). To the Galatians he said: ". . . temperance: against such there is no law. And they that are Christ's have crucified the flesh with the affections and lusts. If we live in the Spirit, let us also walk in the Spirit" (Galatians 5:23–25).

7

The Nocuous Weed

LET US NOW take a look at tobacco, the "nocuous weed." Let me speak first to the teenager or young adult experimenting with cigarettes, in the hope that he will quit before he's hooked.

Why do you smoke? Because you're trying to impress someone? Because your friends do it? Because a sense of security in your relationships depends on it? Because it makes you feel like an adult? Because it gives you the delusion of maturity or sophistication? Perhaps because you are nervous and need a boost to your feeling of self-confidence, or because, in your anxiety, you have to be doing something with your hands? Or have you already gone so far that you're hooked and can't stop? Whatever may be your motivation, smoking is bad news. It is unequivocally indefensible. Nothing can be argued in defense of the filthy habit. It has absolutely no redeeming features.

Smoking gives you a chronic, irritating, dry cough. It makes your breath stink. It makes your clothes reek. It gives you ugly stains on your teeth and fingers. It generally reduces the respect that mature people would otherwise have for you.

It significantly reduces your physical attractiveness to nonsmoking members of the opposite sex. Most of them find the stench of tobacco to be a negative factor in any potential responsiveness to you. If you want to be physically attractive, smelling of stale smoke doesn't exactly help.

You don't like all that I've just said? (I don't blame you, if you are a smoker.) But is it the truth? Do you have these experiences or any sense of guilt about them or wish you could stop the habit? Face reality. It's not too late to change. Smoking hurts no one but you, the smoker, both physically and socially.

Now, to your parents and other adults, let me add this. Consider the medical effects of tobacco upon yourselves.

1. The carbon monoxide in inhaled smoke significantly reduces the ability of hemoglobin in the blood cells to take up oxygen from the lungs and deliver it to the body's tissues.
2. Tests have shown that as few as ten inhalations of smoke increases resistance in the air passages of the lungs, and this choked-up condition persists for an hour after each cigarette.
3. Tiny hairlike cilia, which act as brooms to sweep out the windpipe and bronchial tubes, become paralyzed by smoke, and without this natural defense the lungs become vulnerable to airborne bacteria, viruses, dust particles and chemical pollutants.
4. The lung capacity of habitual smokers gradually shrinks because thickened air sacs throughout the lungs become less efficient in oxygen and carbon-dioxide exchange.
5. Because of tobacco tar in cigarettes, smokers become five times more vulnerable to, and much more affected by, such conditions as chronic bronchitis, emphysema, asthma, and respiratory allergies than do nonsmokers.
6. Nicotine in tobacco is a supertoxic, very lethal poison. As little as five drops can kill an adult. It

acts as rapidly as cyanide. Fortunately, most of it is burned in smoking, but what remains stimulates the sympathetic nervous system, causing it to send more adrenal and other hormones to the heart than it needs. This eventually causes irritation and scarring in the heart muscle, narrowing of the coronary arteries, and a greatly increased chance of blood-clot formation. These conditions eventually end up in a heart attack, and the average age for such victims is getting younger every year.

7. Recent research shows evidence that the combination of smoking and taking birth-control pills reduces the natural resistance of premenopausal women to heart attacks, thereby making them almost as vulnerable as men.

There are potentially dangerous risks for pregnant women who smoke, too. They are more liable to have intrauterine bleeding with fetal death or premature delivery of an underweight baby with an increased chance of its death in the first few months of life.

8. The statistical connection between tobacco tar and lung cancer is so well established now that no other comment is needed. Remember, though, that with its pain, nausea, coughing up blood, weight loss, and partial asphyxiation, having terminal lung cancer is not a very comfortable way to die. The price of a lifetime of smoking is a deathtime of agony.

A word of encouragement: If you give up smoking, almost all toxic effects will disappear within a few weeks, but, of course, destroyed lung tissue can never be regenerated. Some smokers have tried switching to cigars or a pipe, but these are still quite harmful to the lungs, especially if you continue to inhale, though less so than cigarettes. However, they are more likely than cigarettes to cause cancers of the mouth and tongue, because smoke from them is hotter and the concentration of tar is greater. If you can't quit, try to get started on a vigorous physical-conditioning program which will at least help to reduce some of the potential and actual harmful effects of tobacco by increasing lung efficiency and by strengthening the heart.

Let me briefly give you a few scary statistics. If you smoke one twenty-cigarette pack daily, you are eight times more likely to get lung cancer; twenty times more likely with two packs daily than a nonsmoker. Upon discovery of this cancer, only 20 percent are considered operable, and of these only 30 percent or seven people out of a hundred, survive five years. (*See* Appendix D for the American Cancer Society's seven warning signals.)

Smoking's most dangerous effect, statistically, however, is not its effect on the lungs, but on the heart and blood vessels. Sudden death from heart attack has in some instances been found to be as much as sixteen times greater in heavy smokers than nonsmokers. Another study found that the overall death rate from all causes was six times greater in smokers. Life insurance actuarial statistics show that the average fifty-year-old who has smoked one pack daily since age twenty-one has a life expectancy eight and a half years shorter than the nonsmoker. That works out to twenty and one half minutes of life lost for every cigarette!

That's not all. Smokers also incur three times the risk of suffering from a stroke and are twenty times more likely to have disabling constrictions in the arteries of the legs. Blood pressure rises ten to fifteen mm. Hg. in smokers, and they have more peptic ulcers, which heal more slowly. In addition to lung cancer, smokers develop more cancers in the mouth, tongue, lips, esophagus, larynx, pharynx, kidneys, and bladder. Tobacco also has an inhibiting effect on sexual libido. This is often unrecognized by the smoker, who tends to ascribe his lost potency to age or other problems. When he quits smoking, unexpected improvement in this area is a pleasant surprise.

How to quit? It takes motivation and courage. Here are some hopefully helpful suggestions.

There are several systems that use conditioning therapy, with self-imposed rewards for success and penalties for failure. These take several weeks, but work well if you stick with it. The Schick Stop-Smoking Clinics use aversion therapy in which taking certain controlled substances so alters the taste of cigarettes that one quickly loses all desire to smoke again. This is thoroughly unpleasant, but quick and effective.

Hypnosis can sometimes be effective, though I have some reservations. Occasionally, after treatment, an alternative habit may develop, such as nail biting, gum chewing, excessive coffee drinking, or taking tranquilizers, if any underlying problems are not dealt with. Also Christians generally are resistant to the prospect of submitting control of their minds to another person. For these reasons, although I don't recommend a trial of hypnotherapy, I strongly urge anyone intent on giving it a try to go to a well-qualified person, preferably a psychiatrist or other medical doctor.

The department of psychiatry of your local county or city hospital should be able to advise you what number to call to obtain one of these therapies.

"Cold turkey," or ending smoking abruptly by yourself, is the quickest, but the most painful. If you choose this method, pick a definite date: the first of next month, a birthday, an anniversary. It helps the significance of the commitment. Withdrawal symptoms, such as craving, last from two to three weeks, and you may experience temporary nervousness, sleep disturbance, fatigue, slight weight gain, and inability to concentrate. But stick with it. The long-term benefits of quitting far outweigh the brief discomfort period.

Cutting down gradually is less painful, but may take several weeks. In my view this is the best method, if you can be both patient and determined. Use of the four-stage filter system which progressively reduces the tar and nicotine inhaled has helped some to quit over a period of a few weeks. Try also these tested and effective methods which have worked for many who have attended Smoke Enders classes.

1. Realize that smoking is a learned habit and, therefore, through the behavior modification of constant practice, you can relearn the habit of nonsmoking.
2. Motivation is essential. Establish your incentive to quit. Write down a list of reasons: health needs, economics, self-concept, aesthetics, effect on others, example to your children, self-mastery, and so forth. Be positive. Have the attitude that you are achieving something, not that you are denying yourself something.
3. Keep a cigarette count sheet and carefully record every one you use, at what time, under what circumstances, and how you are feeling. Keep the sheet wrapped round your pack and don't light up until you've noted it down.
4. Start breaking the habit by carrying your pack in a different place. At home or in the office store them out of easy reach. Start smoking without inhaling. Hold the cigarette in the hand you don't usually use. Do not carry matches or lighters. Take fewer puffs and use only half the cigarette, or even less. Mix a variety of different brands of cigarettes in your pack. This will begin to make smoking unpleasant.

5. Pick substitute habits to meet needs formerly met by smoking. (This does not include pot, alcohol, or eating!) When you desire a smoke, wait at least five minutes before giving in. Try these distractions first; the desire might go away: Find something small you can play with with your fingers. Take a short but brisk walk, if you can get out. In the office do some isometrics or knee bends. Half a dozen slow, very deep breaths held for a few seconds both at the full and empty points are very therapeutic.

6. Agree with yourself that you will smoke at least one less cigarette tomorrow than today. Again, don't regard this as a sacrifice or feel sorry for yourself. Be glad you're actually succeeding in quitting. The end is in sight. Drink plenty of water to wash the nicotine out of your body.

7. Set a definite date in the near future for your absolute last cigarette. Tell many close friends of your resolve. Such public commitment will bolster your determination. Find a friend who has also successfully quit smoking and encourage each other to stick with it.

8. Committed Christian believers have one additional resource: the power of the indwelling Holy Spirit. "Praise the Lord and Pass the Ammunition" we used to sing in World War II. Any battle in this life needs a combination of personal courage, effort, and determination, with God's invoked strength and help. "God helps those who help themselves" is a well-known, though nonbiblical truism commonly used in our culture. "Fortune favors the brave" is a similar secular motto of a prep school I attended in England.

As Christians, we don't believe in luck, but God so often does seem to bless those who strive to serve Him.

In my life's experience I have found that once I have made my own utmost human effort, somehow things work out for the best eventually. God seems to come through with the answers, and the help. Smoking, (like drinking, overeating, and drug dependence) is a form of lust which can be conquered with a combination of guts and God.

My discipline, motivation and commitment, plus God's support, wisdom, and strength, is an unconquerable team. My part is to ". . . make not provision for the flesh, to fulfil the lusts thereof" (Romans 13: 14). God's part is committed in His promise of Spiritual power: ". . . Walk in the Spirit, and ye *shall not* fulfil the lust of the flesh" (Galatians 5:16, italics added).

A final sobering thought. The graph of cigarette consumption by women has climbed dramatically in the last twenty years, and the graph of their mortality rates from lung cancer and cardiovascular disease has almost exactly paralleled it. It is rapidly approaching the male graph, a doubtful achievement in equality of the sexes. Truly we can say with Virginia Slims, "You've come a long way, baby!"

8

Sweet and Dangerous

HAVING CONSIDERED a few common destructive habits which are totally avoidable, let us now think about one other difficult-to-avoid factor that is involved in the struggle to attain and maintain a healthy body. This is the matter of sugar-filled junk food and its related blood-sugar-imbalance problem which leads to so many physical and emotional symptoms.

First, let's look at junk food. What is it? Junk food is anything that is high in calories but low in nutrition. The two worst criminals in this category, which are commonly eaten in significant quantities by most Americans, are the simple carbohydrates, white flour and refined white sugar. All foods containing these "poisons" as predominant ingredients should be avoided as much as possible. I call them poisons because, even though they do not kill quickly, as arsenic or curare do, they kill in the long run by contributing to obesity, which leads to shortness of breath, high blood pressure, physical weakness, and, eventually, heart failure.

Flour comes from cereal grains, and removal of the outer coat (husk) of the kernel was first practiced by the ancient Egyptians. They found that breads or cakes made from it had a more delicate taste. This refinement was perpetuated as a luxury for the wealthy throughout all subsequent history, until this century. Then, finally, it was realized in 1920 that the discarded outer layer not only contained most of the cereal's vitamins and minerals, but that it was also the best roughage, or natural laxative.

As long ago as 1837 Sylvester Graham (who invented Graham crackers) made the observation that whole-grain food, by providing bulk or fiber in the stool, contributed to regular elimination and was therein a cure for both of the extremes of diarrhea and constipation. We also know today that low-roughage diets are a major factor in the development of lower-gut diverticulitis (weakening and inflammation of the wall), and cancer of the colon and rectum. High fiber/high roughage foods by contrast not only improve elimination, they are probably also a preventive factor in the development of lower-gut cancer.

Unfortunately, however, the 1920s also saw significant good-news and bad-news developments. The "good" was the dramatic increase in availability to the middle classes of refined sugar and white flour at reasonable prices and the exploding popularity of the affordable automobile. This latter, in less than a generation, changed America from a nation of walkers to a nation of riders. The bad news was that, as a direct result of these factors, the incidence of both crippling and fatal heart attacks among middle-aged men began to escalate into the present-day epidemic proportions.

See Appendix E on the effects of excess refined carbohydrates.

Now what are the junk foods to be avoided? Anything made from or containing refined white flour, white rice, or common sucrose sugar. Here are some examples: white bread, pasta (including all types of macaroni noodles such as lasagna and spaghetti), sweetened canned fruits, potato chips, baked goods such as muffins, cakes, pretzels, cookies and other sweets such as pastry, gelatin, candy bars, pie, chocolate, jams, and ice cream. What an insult to your stomach—all that garbage you throw down into it!

Here's more: cola-type drinks, carbonated beverages,

and all other sweetened sodas. Remember also that alcohol in any form is changed into sugar. Then sugar itself: please don't add spoonfuls of it to your coffee, tea, or breakfast cereals. You don't need it. Cut out chewing gum too—it looks terrible! Remember the old joke: "What is the difference between a person chewing gum and a cow chewing grass?" Answer: "The intelligent expression on the cow's face!"

It follows logically for us now to understand the two common diseases related to blood sugar: diabetes and hypoglycemia. After thousands of hours of research work by many physicians and scientists, it was discovered in the early part of this century that the killer disease, diabetes mellitus, was caused by a failure of the pancreas to produce enough of a hormone called insulin. Insulin stimulates the liver to store excess circulating blood glucose in the form of a starch called glycogen. Not enough pancreatic insulin leads to not enough liver-stored glycogen, which leads to too much circulating blood glucose. This is hyperglycemia. *Hyper*glycemia, or *hypo*insulinism, is diabetes. (In Greek *hyper* means "above" or "too much." *Hypo* means "below" or "too little.")

Diabetes is inherited but is usually not manifested until adult life, hence its perpetual transmission from one generation to the next. It is invariably fatal eventually, if untreated, except in its mildest form. Anyone, therefore, with a family history of the condition, who experiences the early symptoms of increased urination, hunger, and thirst now runs to a physician for insulin, knowing his diagnosis. Not so with sufferers from the opposite condition—*hyper*insulinism or *hypo*glycemia.

In hypoglycemia, the pancreas is *too* sensitive. A small rise in blood sugar from eating a candy bar, for example, stimulates an oversecretion of insulin. Up goes the starch glycogen in the liver and down comes the blood sugar. The net result is that the sufferer only feels good for a few minutes before he is hungry again. And he may be more than hungry; there are now recognized to be literally scores of symptoms caused by this up-again-down-again effect on the blood-sugar level. Dozens of diseases have been wrongly diagnosed because of this bewilderingly complex assortment of subjective experiences.

Doctors Cheraskin and Ringsdorf in their excellent book, *Psychodietetics*, give a thorough list all of us should think through in case we might be among the estimated 20 million people in this country believed to have this often misdiagnosed and, therefore, improperly treated condition. They state:

An abnormal plunge in blood sugar levels is perilous, sending shock waves through every cell in the body and affecting the nervous system and the brain most of all. An erratic mental state results, with a list of symptoms and complaints reading like a compendium on a bottle of snake-oil medicine: dizziness, fainting or blackouts, headaches, fatigue or exhaustion, drowsiness, narcolepsy (abnormal attacks of sleepiness), muscle pains and cramps, cold hands and feet, numbness, insomnia, nightmares, irritability, crying spells, restlessness, nervous breakdown, inability to concentrate, excessive worry and anxiety, depression, forgetfulness, illogical fears, suicidal thoughts, tremors, cold sweats, inner trembling, uncoordination, convulsion, fast and/or noticeable heart beat, blurred vision, allergies, itching and crawling sensations, neurodermatitis, arthritic pains, gastrointestinal upsets, loss of appetite, loss of sexual drive, and impotency.

Spells of low blood sugar give rise to other widely assorted difficulties: dry or burning mouth, ringing in the ears, poor memory, temper tantrums, noise and light sensitivity, shortness of breath, peculiar breath or perspiration odor, nausea, and hot flashes.

A typical hypoglycemia victim is, in fact, an emotional yo-yo, strung out on a chemical reaction he cannot control, with reactions so severe they frequently resemble insanity.

With such a variety of symptoms, it is not surprising that many sufferers confuse and frustrate their family physicians, who are at a loss to identify and treat the disease. Their friends and families also lose patience with their complaints, accusing them of being hypochondriacs or neurotics. But, fortunately, there is a good test available to expose hypoglycemia, and most competent physicians nowadays can arrange for it to be done if the condition is suspected. This is called the six-hour glucose tolerance test. (*See* Appendix F.)

Now what can we do about sugar-imbalance problems? Remember, we are not considering only those people who have an established hypoglycemia condition, but *anyone* who has experienced any of the above-mentioned symptoms, or is concerned not to develop them. This hopefully should include everyone! Eating any quick, junk-food calories is the worst thing one can do. Junk foods stimulate blood-sugar imbalance and a condition of malnourishment. Millions of people who should know better live on a constant intake of high carbohydrates. They feel good for half an hour, and then another slump hits!

No, blood-sugar levels should be built up *gradually,* not suddenly: That's the key. Blood-sugar (glucose) levels are built up slowly and maintained for long periods by regularly eating a fully nutritional diet, balanced to meet all the body's metabolic needs. A balanced diet is the subject of the next chapter.

9

You Are What You Eat

Now, WHAT about a balanced diet that will not cause yo-yoing blood-sugar levels, will not be too fattening, yet will be adequate in all nutritional needs? Answers coming up—but, first, a few warnings.

Read the labels on all the canned and processed foods you buy. Try to avoid any containing additives, artificial coloring or flavoring, sweeteners, stabilizers, emulsifiers or preservatives such as nitrates or nitrites. Many large-volume supermarket foods sold in prepackaged containers or cartons include some of these foreign substances. Admittedly it is sometimes slightly more expensive, but you are really much better off going to a grocery or health-food store for such basics as fresh fruits, raw vegetables, and whole-grain cereals.

There is also another kind of food which it is best to avoid because it is really a drug, an artificial stimulant. It is caffeine. Caffeine is found in chocolate, cocoa, tea, all cola drinks, and, worst of all, in coffee. Caffeine stimulates the production of adrenalin, a hormone produced in the adrenal glands, and this in turn stimulates the release of glucose from liver glycogen, thereby raising the blood-sugar level. This stimulates insulin production, and we're back in our vicious circle again. Small amounts of these drinks are okay, if they are spaced apart, but never have more than two cups of coffee at any one meal or snack, and try not to have more than five in any one day.

Also, don't be fooled by labels claiming that bread, breakfast cereals, or other baked goods are *supplemented, enriched,* or *fortified.* Of the twenty-odd vitamins, minerals, and amino acids removed from whole wheat in the making of white flour, only four or five are returned. Stick with high-fiber, whole-grain breads and cereals.

Avoid hydrogenated (saturated) fats such as are commonly found in solid cooking fat and coffee lighteners. Cook and eat all animal meats as lean as possible. Refined vegetable oils tend to be saturated and not good, whereas corn oil, peanut oil, cottonseed oil, and safflower-seed oil tend to be unrefined and, therefore, unsaturated.

Extra salt should be avoided. In cooking, use only what is necessary to produce pleasurable taste. Sprinkling on extra tends to cause fluid retention in excess of the body's hydration needs. Brown or *raw* sugars are not much better than white sugar. They are still sucrose. If you must satisfy your sweet tooth, use a small amount of honey. It is twice as sweet as sugar, and the fructose in it uses less insulin for its metabolism.

That's enough of what not to eat: What then *should* we eat? There is still much good food available to us. Pin this list to your kitchen bulletin board. It is the opinion of many nutritionists and dietitians that we should eat liberally of the following:

1. Veal, poultry, and fish are excellent. Have at least one of these every day.
2. Beef, lamb, and pork are also high in protein value, but cut off as much of the fat on them as possible. Two or three times weekly should be enough of them.
3. Eggs, cheese, and milk are also high in nutrients. Use them daily.
4. Fruit, vegetables, and their juices are high in vita-

mins, minerals, and fiber bulk. Again, they should be taken every day without fail.

5. Breads and cereals, as mentioned, should be of the whole-wheat variety. Use only very moderate quantities, since they are carbohydrates.
6. Nuts and seeds supply essential fatty acids and some proteins.
7. Gravy and sauces should not contain too much fat or flour. Margarine is preferable to butter.

If, for variety, you must take some "forbidden" foods, be disciplined and take them only occasionally and in small quantities.

A couple of quick points about cholesterol, a fatty substance notorious for being deposited on the interior linings of the coronary arteries, thereby setting up conditions for a heart attack. Only 20 percent of all the cholesterol in the body comes from dietary intake such as meats, dairy produce, shellfish, and eggs. The rest is manufactured in the liver and in other body cells from acetate radicles. These are found in high quantities—in what? You've guessed it—in refined sugar! Also eggs are rich in lecithin, which actually controls and even lowers cholesterol levels, a providential balance mechanism. Cutting out eggs and so forth and thereby reducing dietary cholesterol intake can actually be counterproductive, because the less there is in the diet, the more the body will make for itself. So go ahead and enjoy a couple of eggs daily, if you like them, but junk the junk!

It has also been discovered recently that people with a high ratio of high-density lipoproteins (HDLs) are protected from heart attacks, even if their blood cholesterol level is high. This is because these HDLs carry cholesterol back to the liver for excretion, thereby reducing arterial deposits. Who has high HDL ratios? Vegetarians, marathon runners, and those lucky enough to have been born that way. So if inheritance didn't help you and you don't want to become a vegetarian, you can at least exercise. You don't actually have to run marathons, though. Tests on medical students in New Orleans showed that vigorous exercise for thirty to forty minutes, four times per week, soon started to raise their HDLs to protective levels.

Now what about nutritional supplements? I am not a health-food nut, but I do recognize that even a diet taken as just recommended might sometimes be deficient in certain essential nutrients (if, for example, insufficient amounts of fruits and vegetables were taken). In addition to plenty of proteins, fats, and carbohydrates, which you will automatically get from a balanced diet, remember the vitamins and minerals we all need daily. See Appendix G for a list of sources of all essential vitamins. If you can see from this appendix that your intake is deficient in any area, you can quickly know in what ways it should be supplemented. City and suburban dwellers in this country, who do not have ready access to the fresh local produce of rural areas, probably will find that they will need to take some vitamins and minerals in tablet or other form regularly. (Synthetically produced tablets are almost always just as nutritionally efficacious as more expensive "natural" foods, many of which have synthetic supplements in them anyway.)

Finally, how should we eat? Most experienced nutritionists, from what I have read, would recommend something like this:

1. *Have a good breakfast.* I was appalled, on arriving in this country, to discover that coffee and a Danish was the extent of many Americans' breakfasts. Having usually eaten nothing since supper, ten to twelve hours earlier, they have a very low blood-sugar level at 7:00 A.M. Then what? A hunk of junk and some caffeine. Up goes the blood glucose level, out comes the insulin like a protective lioness, and

way down goes the glucose again. By 10:00 or 11:00 A.M. it's hypoglycemia time, with all its frayed nerves, depression, anxiety, hostility, and regrettable speech or behavior!

What is the answer to this? Yes, the low blood sugar has to be elevated to meet the waking day's need for calorific expenditure, but it should be done with a full, balanced meal, not a quick, temporary drug and junk stimulus. I personally recommend for breaking the fast something like eggs, sausages, or bacon, orange juice, whole-wheat cereal or bread, and tea (less caffeine than coffee). Take your multivitamin pill at this time or with the evening meal.

Breakfast should be the largest meal of the day and the only one after which it's okay to feel comfortably full. You have all day to burn up all the ingested calories so that they will not be converted into fat deposits.

2. *Avoid midmorning junk snack.* Cup of coffee if you have to, but only one. (Remember: milk is okay, but no sugar!) Fruit juice however is much preferable, or a cup of hot bouillon. Don't be pressured by your co-workers into dumping several hundred calories into your system. The infamous tradition of the coffee break has killed more Americans than the automobile: And it's not so much the coffee itself, it's all the cookies and pastries that go with it.

3. *Eat a light lunch, most preferably of the salad type.* This should be high in fresh vegetables or fruit—good both for bulk fiber and for vitamins and minerals.

4. *Don't indulge in an afternoon junk snack.* No one needs it. Get your day's work finished, instead!

5. *Enjoy a good supper or dinner between 6:00 and 8:00 P.M., not later.* This is usually the day's hot, cooked-protein meal, of substantial meat and veg-

etables. Make sure that all your nutritional needs
are met by adding to this meal any nutrients known
to be deficient. Quality not quantity is the key here.
Eating a heavy meal, regularly, just before going to
bed, puts on weight inexorably. Let your supper be
of high nutritional value, well controlled in
amount, and not too late in the evening.

A final word for mothers about small children who can
only handle three small meals daily and need two or
three between-meal snacks. The suggestions given previously about not snacking only apply to fully grown
adults, the people who have stopped growing taller and
are now growing fatter! Children are different, even up
to late adolescence.

Meal times need to be sensibly planned to meet children's different needs. Because of their high energy/
high calorific expenditure, it is appropriate for them to
have more carbohydrates than adults, but they still need
to be protected from too many sugary foods, which they
naturally like. Give your energetic child all the carbohydrates he needs, preferably in the form of baked
potatoes, rice, wheat bread, and unrefined cereals. Try to
train him, however, to restrict rigidly his intake of candy,
ice cream, salty snack foods, cookies, and sweetened
sodas. Check with your pediatrician for a weight chart
for different ages of children. In our culture, being
overweight is a much more common problem in children
than malnutrition.

Between-meal snacks should preferably be of such
items as cheese, crackers, celery, carrot sticks, fresh fruit
and juices, and milk. Make these readily available for
them to help themselves from the refrigerator, but don't
even permit any junk food in the house. Remember, a fat
child becomes a fat adolescent, who becomes a fat adult.
Dietary discipline in youth will lead to greater ability to
control one's intake in adulthood and thereby obviate
much misery in later years.

10

Relaxation and Sleep

ALL OF CREATION is in a constant state of alternating periods of high and low energy output. The entire universe is presently expanding. One theory has it that eventually it will contract and then expand and contract again, and so on, perhaps forever. Many of the cosmic electromagnetic radiations that reach us from outer space are pulsating. The sun alternates periods of more and less heat radiation. The tilt of the earth, relative to its plane of orbit around the sun, gives us our alternating hot and cold seasons.

Biology is no different. Many animals hibernate through the winter and become reactivated in the spring. The earth alternates its day and night cycle, with man and most other living things adjusting activity levels accordingly. Sleep is part of the cycle of life, and, in adult humans, should occupy about one third of it: But, during waking hours, most people also need periods of alternating relaxation from the stress of daily duties.

Stress is unavoidable for most people, especially those with pressured city-business life-styles, though country folk also experience some different forms of stress. Although some people experience anxiety without stress, the vast bulk of human suffering in the form of nervous tension or apprehension is caused by the various emotional stresses and strains of daily living. Generally speaking, stress is worse in this generation than in most previous ones. The pace of life in this twentieth century is certainly much more stressful for most people than it was a hundred years ago.

Urban living is generally more stressful than suburban or country living. The hostility, rudeness, and selfish behavior in crowds is inevitable in cities. Noise is very stressful. Fire and police sirens, construction and repair squads with compressed-air drills, trucks and motorcycles, buses and subways—all add to the constant stress of city life. The poor have anxiety about how to make ends meet, but the rich are anxious about their investments, business deals, and the state of the market. Performing well on the job and getting on well with the boss or fellow workers can also be very stressful. Unemployment and physical illness are great threats to one's tranquility. Hatred, boredom, frustration, and fatigue are common causes of internal stress.

Stress is the wear and tear of life, but it is not the stress itself but the effects it produces on our bodies and minds that are damaging. Some stresses are good. A game of tennis, a thrilling movie, or an exciting, happy piece of news are stresses which, like anxiety, cause rapid heartbeat, but they are not damaging, in reasonable quantities. Some stress is necessary. We are at our least stressful on first waking in the morning. We have poor physical coordination and some mental confusion, initially, but the stress of having to get up and dressed for the day helps us to pull ourselves together quickly.

We all have to live with stress, which is defined by Dr. Hans Selye of Montreal as the nonspecific response of the body to any demand made upon it. Stress is not in itself harmful to the body or mind, unless it is too severe, lasts too long, recurs too frequently, or is not alternated with periods of adequate relaxation. By contrast, stress which is too severe, protracted, recurrent, and unrelieved leads to definite physiological effects on the body.

The commonest biological defensive reaction to stress is an increased outpouring of adrenaline and other hormones from the adrenal glands. This is known as the biologic stress reaction and leads to a condition now commonly called "the general adaptation syndrome." This is manifested in two distinct groups of symptoms, the immediate and the delayed, the acute and the chronic.

The acute results are such effects as raised blood-sugar level (*see* chapter eight), raised blood pressure, increased pulse and respiration rate, and other signs such as sweating, dilated pupils, and subjective feelings of anxiety. Added together, these results are known as the "fight-or-flight" response. This primitive defensive reaction to protect from danger is essential to life. Without it, man and animals would never have survived.

If, however, the stress or stresses on the organism continue beyond the acute episode, there follows a period of attempted adjustment. The success or failure of the adjustment depends on the severity and continuity of the stressor and the adaptive ability of the one being stressed. Adaptation, however, can lead to many well-recognized secondary diseases, some of them more painful to the sufferer than the original stress. Best known of these are high blood pressure, heart attacks, gastric ulcers, allergic reactions, and such neurotic conditions as anxiety attacks and depressive mood swings.

Remember, however, that stress is not all bad. It can be the spice of life. Life would be terribly boring without frequent moderately stressful events. (*See* Appendix H on stress scales of adjustments to change.) We need the stimulus of moderate and frequent, but not constant, stress. Work is a form of stress, whether it be in an office, a shop, or in the home. Doctor Selye teaches that hard work is a biological necessity both for personal happiness and for a long, satisfying, and successful life.

The key to the balance, however, and therefore the key to a health-giving life-style, is the well-disciplined, constant alternation of stress with relaxation. We need both. The stress of unemployment is boredom and frustration. The person who has no regular daily work or occupation must find some alternative activity to fulfill his needs for the expenditure of both physical and intellectual energy. If he does not find some such outward expression, his very inactivity can lead to the same stress reactions as the overworked person.

It is hard to define work and play. One definition is that work is what we have to do; play is what we want to do. Happy, indeed, therefore, is the person who thoroughly enjoys his work, and sad by contrast is the person who has no satisfying or enjoyable play or leisure activity. Disliking your work and having no fun in life are both very stressful. They have different causes, but the same results.

The biologic rhythm of stress and relaxation, of work and play, of activity and rest is essential to health. The unemployed must find work or some other satisfying commitment from which he can derive a sense of personal fulfillment. The hard worker needs some regular means of dissipating his pent-up energies, hostilities, anxieties, and frustrations. If he does not meet this need, he will eventually develop some of the signs and symptoms of the general stress syndrome.

How then can we relax? What should we do to develop this balance in our lives? What really is relaxation?

Relaxation is not the same as inactivity. It is not doing nothing. It is doing something different, or creating a change of pace in one's life. An ideal vacation, in my view, is not one spent lying on a beach all day, getting sunburned. It is, rather, going to new places, doing new things, meeting new people, earning new ideas, or even new philosophies. Releasing tension is an essential part of the cycle of life. It is good to stop the pace of life frequently and allow time for thinking, for meditating, for daydreaming, for reading things of interest, for pursuing hobbies, games, and sports, doing relaxation exercises, even for having a little cry occasionally. A great doctor once said, "The sorrow that has no vent in tears will make other organs weep." In other words, it is better to have a good cry than to develop high blood pressure or a stomach ulcer. However you do it, relaxing from the stress of your daily routine is essential and must be done regularly. The biological cycle of alternating activity and rest is an integral part of maintaining bodily health and emotional stability.

Many people have different ideas on what is best for them to achieve relaxation and produce inner tranquility and peace of mind. I personally have successfully tried three totally different, but all very effective, methods—one spiritual, one physical, and one psychological.

As a Christian, my daily times of personal prayer and devotional Bible study, most effectively enjoyed at the beginning of the day, prepare me for the stresses of my work. I am much better able to handle the intellectual challenges and the emotional pressures of my daily work as a psychiatrist, if I have had my first session of the day alone with God.

Regular strenuous physical exercise I also find essential, not only to bodily health, but also to the preservation of a mind at peace with man and God. Playing squash or running six days every week enables me to work out of my system any bottled-up anger, impatience, frustration, or anxiety. (More on this in chapters thirteen and fourteen.)

Psychological relaxation has been practiced in both Eastern and Western cultures for centuries. Meditational techniques of yoga and Zen Buddhism have demonstrated for thousands of years many people's remarkable ability to gain control over the mind and certain other physiological functions which can lead to profound mental and physical relaxation. Transcendental Meditation (TM), recently popularized in the USA by Maharishi Mahesh Yogi, is an old yogic technique adapted to be acceptable to the Western mind.

Some years ago, for professional reasons, in order more practically to understand the problem of how best to relax, an important part of my teaching psychotherapy to those needing it, I paid my money and went through the initiation ceremony and beginner's training of TM. I was given by my teacher a personal, secret *mantra,* a meaningless sound upon which I was to focus my attention and repeat over and over while meditating. I was somewhat shocked and uncomfortably embarrassed however, to discover that the initiation was actually some form of Eastern religious ceremony. I also found that I simply could not readjust my daily schedule to devoting two periods of twenty to thirty minutes, morning and evening, to its practice. So I quit.

However, several months later, I read the excellent little paperback, *The Relaxation Response,* by Herbert Benson, a professor of medicine at Harvard. Doctor Benson has painstakingly examined many meditation methods, and states that the same results as TM can be achieved, without any religious overtones, by fulfilling four basic conditions. If these conditions are met for ten to twenty minutes daily, great relaxation is experienced and more energy and acuteness apparently become available for any physical or mental activity which follows.

Doctor Benson's four conditions are:

1. A quiet environment.
2. A comfortable position (in an armchair is probably the best).

3. A passive attitude (of "let it happen" and "don't be bothered by distracting thoughts").
4. A mental device. This could be any sound or word, which should be repeated over and over again. The word *one* is a sufficiently adequate sound to focus upon to achieve good relaxation. An alternative could be any object upon which to fix one's gaze. Either of these merely help the mind to shift away from logical, externally oriented thought to conscious awareness of the ever-deepening relaxation of all the muscles of the body.

I do not practice this meditation regularly, but I have found that something similar to Dr. Benson's technique is very helpful occasionally. If, for example, I get a headache, become very worried about something, lose my concentration at work, or if I'm becoming very anxious about having too many things to do all at once, I find that a brief period of meditation is very calming. I find I only need about five to seven minutes of this type of nonreligious meditation to achieve a beautiful sense of relaxation in both body and mind, after which I can get on with dealing with my responsibilities.

Two words of caution: first, for Christians. There is for some the question of what might happen if they allow their minds to drift away from conscious control. Some have voiced fears that they would be exposing themselves to demonic intrusion if they were not at all times in contact with the external reality of their immediate environment. This has never been a problem for me. I know that, for me, my mind is in control at all times, and I have never experienced any demonic influence. I also know both by faith and by experience that He that is within me, God's Holy Spirit, is far too powerful to permit any evil influence to enter my mind and soul for as long as I remain faithful to Him.

Second, as a psychiatrist, I have serious reservations about recommending the relaxation-response technique to anyone who is mentally or emotionally unstable. Those with a very low self-image or poor reality contact might not be able to experience the benefits without some confusion. So, if you have any serious psychological or spiritual problems, better not use this technique. If, however, you are healthy, it can be an occasional, useful adjunct to your prayer and exercise practices to maintain peace and calmness within.

What about your sleep? If you get too little, consistently, over many weeks, it may adversely affect you both physically and emotionally. Severe insomnia for extended periods can lead to disorders of thought and perception that are similar to some of the symptoms seen in acute schizophrenia, the most serious of the mental illnesses.

Newborn babies sleep up to sixteen hours every day, but this amount rapidly decreases through infancy. Teenagers and children every day need about nine hours sleep. Young adults need eight hours, middle-aged people seven, and elderly folk six hours every day, though senior citizens can sometimes also benefit from an additional afternoon nap, if they get very tired. As you get older, your basal metabolic rate falls, and you get by with less sleep.

Sleep researchers have discovered that even within an average seven- to eight-hour night there is an approximately ninety-minute sleep cycle. About every one and one half hours throughout the night, a normal person experiences REM sleep, lasting a few minutes. REM stands for Rapid Eye Movements, a trembling of the eyeballs, which can be observed under the sleeper's eyelids. REM sleep is associated with dreaming and occurs four or five times during the night, the later ones, during the lighter sleep of the early morning hours, being slightly longer. This ninety-minute cycle corresponds with the basic biological rest-activity rhythmicity associated with waxing and waning within the central nervous system.

Some common causes of insomnia are:

1. Discomfort due to noise, light, an uncomfortable bed, physical illness, or extremes of external temperature or humidity.
2. Inability to unwind and forget the day's stresses, fears, pressures, apprehensions, or anxiety caused by overwork or worry.
3. Depression of mood in any form which can cause difficulty in getting to sleep, staying asleep, or cause early morning waking.
4. Guilt, denial, and other protective psychological defense mechanisms which either prevent sleep altogether or repress conscious thoughts into the unconscious mind, which then resurrects them in the form of unpleasant dreams and nightmares.
5. Extended jet travel, especially from West to East, across several time zones.
6. Poor physical fitness associated with not enough exercise, resulting in inadequate general muscular tiredness and need for rest. Tired mind and muscles guarantee a good night's sleep. (*See* chapters thirteen and fourteen.) Athletes and people in good physical condition usually sleep well and arise refreshed. People in poor shape often sleep fitfully and tend to get drowsy in the afternoon.

Your eight hours minimum sleep should preferably be had during darkness. It is more healthy to be up and about when the sun is up. In other words, let your sleep be from 11:00 P.M. to 7:00 A.M. rather than from 3:00 A.M to 11:00 A.M.! Habitual late nights are not good for general health. This "day-night reversal" involving lying in long hours in the morning can lead to decadence, lazy habits, and avoidance of responsibilities. It also is sometimes an early indication of mental illness.

The following prebedtime habits can help to ensure good sleep regularly:

1. Avoid caffeine in any form after 6:00 or 7:00 P.M.
2. Avoid either strenuous exercise or a large meal within two hours of going to bed.
3. Relax in a deep armchair or a hot tub within an hour of sleep.
4. A hot milk drink is an excellent relaxant for both body and mind.
5. Sexually well-adjusted married couples often find that they sleep deeper and longer if they have intercourse immediately before going to sleep.
6. Sleep medications should only be taken as an absolute last resort, especially by anyone under sixty years of age. In any event, take them only if your physician suggests them. If he does, ask him to prescribe a nonbarbiturate which does not cause hangovers or addiction. Do *not* mix any sedatives with alcohol.
7. Prayer before retiring can also help achieve a natural deep sleep. Committing worries, fears, and guilt feelings to God, confessing and repenting of sins and accepting forgiveness for them, trusting that He will take care of tomorrow as He has today, and just fully resting in God's loving and protective care, bring a deep peace to both mind and spirit. "I will both lay me down in peace, and sleep: for thou, Lord, only makest me dwell in safety" (Psalms 4:8).

11

Sex—Who Needs It?

SEX—WHO NEEDS IT? Or, rather, who *thinks* he needs it? Here is at least a partial answer: He or she who "needs" it is he or she who has become accustomed to it. As with so many things in life, actions lead to habits, and habits lead to cravings for more actions.

This is not a book devoted to theology, philosophy, practical Christianity, social morality, or ethics. It is concerned with bodily well-being, and I am simply asking the question as to whether sexual activity is needful for it. The answer you get to the question depends on whom you ask.

The celibate, or sexually unaroused, adult male or female might be able, truthfully, to claim that he or she has been able to remain in good physical condition without any sexual activity. If you ask him or her, however, about the effects of adult celibacy on his or her *emotional* well-being, answers will vary from confession of acute frustration or anxiety at one extreme, to total equanimity, with peaceful acceptance of the deprivation, at the other.

The fact of human experience is that we are different. Many people can go through life with no sexual experiences, even in fantasy; many others seem to be in constant need of both emotional and genital expression and fulfillment. "If you've never had it, you don't miss it" is an old saying, and one that is as true for sexual craving as for any other desire or need.

Sexually, we differ. Some apparently have a much greater craving and need for sexual activity than others. Some, for example, are able to make a lifetime commitment to celibacy. Some are easily able to be faithful to one marital partner. But some others find it almost impossible not to desire a variety of sexual partners. Christians are no different in terms of their varying natures and appetites. They *are* different, of course, in both the motivation and ability they possess to control their natural cravings.

Sadly however most Christians do not develop or fully utilize this potential, and thereby remain undisciplined in mind and body. This so often leads to consuming guilt, anxiety, and depression of mood which cripple the joy in the Christian experience and can destroy emotional health. God does not give easy victory over sexual sins or any other sins. He does, however, give power to help the Christian who is prepared to suffer the pain of the struggle.

The main theme of this book, however, is not the rights and wrongs of sexual morality, but the consideration of the body's health needs. A healthy body, though, is closely integrated with a healthy mind. For this reason, emotional problems such as anxiety, guilt, or frustration caused by sexual problems or attitudes can adversely affect the healthy functioning of the physical body. Let us therefore briefly consider the matter of sexual activity as either a contributor to or a detractor from bodily well-being and general health. I will not, however, totally evade matters of Christian morality. Issues such as guilt and sublimation are relevant to this book and will be mentioned later in this chapter.

Let us first consider married couples. In the first book of the Bible we read, "And God blessed them, and God said unto them, Be fruitful, and multiply . . ." (Genesis 1:28). In the next chapter is written, "Therefore shall a man leave his father and his mother, and shall cleave unto his wife: and they shall be one flesh." The next verse states, "And they were both naked, the man and his wife, and were not ashamed" (Genesis 2:24, 25).

In response to a letter from Corinth, the apostle Paul wrote:

> Nevertheless to avoid fornication, let every man have his own wife, and let every woman have her own husband. Let the husband render unto the wife due benevolence [love]: and likewise also the wife unto the husband. The wife hath not power of her own body, but the husband: and likewise also the husband hath not power of his own body, but the wife. Defraud ye not one the other, except it be with consent [mutual agreement] for a time . . . .
> 1 Corinthians 7:2–5

From these Scriptures, we understand that in God's eyes the purposes of the gift of sex within marriage are threefold:

1. Continuing propagation of the species
2. Mutual satisfaction of sexual needs
3. Reciprocal expression of commitment and love for each other

These three principles lead us to understand three instinctual drives: the reproductive, the physiological, and the emotional. As just stated, the last two of these are closely related and are our concern in this book.

Whereas it is possible for most healthy people to remain physically fit without sexual activity, there are, nevertheless, certain respects in which meeting of sexual and emotional needs do contribute to one's total well-being. For example: It has been the discovery of many married couples that having intercourse after going to bed at night enables them to fall asleep more quickly and to sleep more soundly, due to the total relaxation that usually follows orgasm.

By contrast, sexual deprivation or lack of satisfaction, for whatever reason, can lead to emotional disturbances such as anxiety, depression, resentment, frustration, anger, guilt, hostility, frigidity, or impotence. These symptoms are characteristic of many of the shaky or frankly disintegrating Christian marriages I see daily in my practice. Middle-aged male impotence is often caused by the man's body being unfit. It can also be caused through his wife's inability any longer to excite him. Even the prettiest young girl starts to sag and slump as she gets older, and unless she keeps herself in good physical shape, her overweight, bulging stomach and hips will be likely to turn off her husband's desire towards her. His own unfitness also can of course lead to her frigidity. A fit body is an attractive body.

Emotional responses (for example, to sexual rejection) can lead to such physical manifestations as appetite changes leading to significant weight gain or loss, development of gastric ulceration, high blood pressure, colitis with diarrhea, skin disorders, insomnia, and a variety of other psychosomatic manifestations.

Sexual intercourse within marriage, therefore, should be enjoyed as frequently as it is mutually pleasurable, and should be refrained from only, as Paul recommended, "with consent for a time."

Now, for single people: The comments above referring to the emotional and physiological effects of sexual deprivation in marriage are, of course, for the most part, as true for singles, once they become sexually active, as for married people. If not genitally, certainly emotionally, any healthy adult experiences some sexual, or at least affectional, needs. (These are the needs to love and be loved.)

A single person who has experienced sexual enjoyment or fulfillment before marriage may develop a continuing craving for both the sexual and affectional satisfaction such relationships can bring. When these satisfactions cannot be met, for whatever reason, there is the tragic possibility of the development of resentment, bitterness, jealousy, and feelings of rejection and loneliness. These emotions, in turn, can lead to some of the physical problems just indicated, which are definitely harmful to bodily health.

By contrast, single people who have never been sexually active, and therefore have not developed the habit of obtaining sexual satisfaction, whether by intercourse or masturbation, seem better able to go through life without strong cravings for sexual activity. This is rare, however, especially in men.

Although most parents still hope that their daughters are virgins on their wedding days, the fact is that mature but sexually unaroused women are approaching the endangered-species list. The sexual needs of women have long been underrated and, until recent times, underresearched. Most people in our society today realize that it is healthy and normal for a woman to enjoy sex as much as a man. She may no longer be as satisfied to take a passive role in the sex act, as were, for example, many women in her grandmothers' generation. Women now often participate and enjoy sex equally with men, though they usually need, more than men, the security of a committed relationship.

Furthermore, in one generation, we have experienced the development of sexual permissiveness in Western culture, which was undreamed of a few years ago. We have also witnessed the emergence of the women's liberation movement, the breakdown of the double standard, the change of attitude toward virginity, the easy access of birth-control methods, legalized abortion, and the single-parent family.

In spite of these powerful influences, however, some women still choose, for moral or religious reasons, to remain chaste and to keep themselves for their future husbands. Such a woman will, of course, have emotional needs for love and companionship, and she will be obliged, therefore, to find ways to meet these needs from sources other than from a husband or lover. The same holds true for men, of course, but because of the much easier availability of casual sex for males and their usually much more intense genital cravings, their motivation for chastity, and the strength to achieve it, generally need to be very much more disciplined.

If, for the present, marriage seems not to be your lot, you can still achieve some measure of peace within yourself and in your relationships by the development of attitudes of sublimation. Sublimation consists of diverting the energy of sexual drives and the cravings for affectional needs into alternative satisfying and fulfilling pursuits. Total diversion is of course neither possible nor even needful. Sublimation can, however, reduce or take the edge off the acuteness of the pain of unfulfilled desires in these areas. It is basically a healthy defense mechanism. Repression, by contrast, which is the attempt to forget or deny one's needs, is unhealthy, unrealistic, and can lead to anxiety or depression. In our culture, both men and women can become actively involved in vocational, avocational, religious, social, cultural, or sporting pursuits which can satisfy many emotional needs. Single people who have successfully achieved such diversions can realistically function happily without a mate, even for a lifetime.

A major personal problem about which there is a real division among Christians is the question as to whether or not masturbation is a sin. I have found very little written in any Christian books which can be of help to unnecessarily guilt-ridden young people agonizing over this matter. Read an excellent book on this called *My Beautiful Feeling* by Walter Trobisch.

I have a close friend who has told me that he never masturbated and very rarely even felt the urge to do so. He is now happily married, considers his sex life to be normal, and has no extramarital activities or fantasies. I know one or two single priests and nuns who have made lifetime commitments to celibacy, and since their unwavering mental attitudes are that all sexual activity is permanently off limits, they say they are not troubled by sexual temptations. Such saints really exist, but they must be extremely rare. I'm not sure if I envy them or feel sorry for them. I *am* sure that for the majority of Christians, complete chastity is not God's calling for their personal lives, marriage, of course, being the only biblical provision for meeting sexual needs.

Masturbation, now known to be almost as common in women as in men, can provide some measure of temporary reduction of internal tension. In the case of women, though their physical well-being may not require it, most who have been sexually aroused need some sexual or at least some affectional fulfillment for their emotional well-being and stability. In our culture, often, emotional needs for love and companionship, though present, tend not to be as much of a source of craving for a man as for a woman. On the other hand, a man's genital sexual needs somehow tend to be more acute than that of most women, probably because they are more physiologically bound.

In the adolescent and adult male, from puberty to advanced old age, sperm are constantly being manufactured by the testicles, transported towards the base of the bladder, mixed with fluid secreted by the prostate gland, and stored in two small sacs called seminal vesicles. Some absorption takes place, but this rarely, if ever, keeps pace with production, especially in younger men. Sooner or later, the vesicles become full and their contents need to be discharged. If this does not happen through intercourse or masturbation, it will occur spontaneously, during sleep. This nocturnal emission is often associated with an erotic dream and, without other sexual activity, will normally occur every two or three weeks.

Much more often, however, a male does not experience these emissions, because his sexual cravings tend to lead to intercourse or masturbation long before the vesicles are full. One cannot say dogmatically that the regular ejaculation of seminal fluid is essential to the body's physical well-being. It does seem, however, that attempts to resist the urge to masturbate, for both sexes, can lead to increasing anxiety and inner tension in those used to its regular practice.

Another problem to be faced is that of the guilt which almost always develops in those who have been taught that masturbation is morally wrong or sinful. I can feel and suffer with them. I have lived through this myself. Single to the age of thirty-seven, I know what it is like to live for twenty years as an adult male, struggling with healthy and natural desires for sexual gratification. Far from claiming to be sin-free, I have, nevertheless, personally experienced the fiery conflict within of the "ought to" versus the "want to," the spiritual versus the carnal, that Paul describes so vividly: "For the good that I would I do not: but the evil which I would not, that I do" (Romans 7:19). Like Paul, I have experienced both defeats and victories.

I have, therefore, two key thoughts to share with any

young person now going through what I have been
through:

First, there is no question that one's sexual drives can
be at least partially diverted into other channels. For me
there were three:

1. Intense academic study for many years, developing
    my professional career. (For the creative rather
    than scholarly person it could be art, music and so
    forth.)
2. Extensive physical activities, recreational pursuits,
    and sporting endeavors several times each week.
3. Religious commitments of preaching or teaching,
    and the disciplined pursuit of my personal spiritual
    development, which necessitated hundreds of
    hours of private prayer and devotional Bible study
    during my formative years. I permitted myself very
    few idle moments. An idle mind easily gravitates to
    sensuous thoughts.

Second, I kept short accounts with God. I never let
unrepented sin remain as a barrier between me and my
Lord. Failure to have victory over any temptation or sin
was at once confessed so that fellowship could be immediately restored. Nor have I ever allowed the cer-
tainty of future sin to become a barrier. It was a matter of
living one day at a time, trusting God to provide for all
one's needs, whether it was the need for strength to conquer, or the need for forgiveness and encouragement
after failure.

There have been times when the temptations of the
flesh seemed to be more than one could bear. These are
not easy times, nor is there a simple solution to find
relief if one chooses to live within the parameters of
Christian principles. I have found prayer is invariably a
comfort and source of needed power. It helps one

through the darkest hours of loneliness and frustration, and it provides light in the darkness. I am always helped, also, by these words of Paul, "There hath no temptation taken you but such as is common to man: but God is faithful, who will not suffer you to be tempted above that ye are able; but will with the temptation also make a way to escape, that ye may be able to bear it" (1 Corinthians 10:13).

We are creatures of habit, and most sex practices in and out of marriage are developed between couples in conformity with habitual actions or needs. The celibate habitually excludes sexually tempting thoughts, and for him practice makes perfect. He who habitually masturbates yields easily whenever the urge hits him, and ceasing the practice becomes harder the more often it has happened. Married couples develop habitual sex practices which are mutually pleasurable or satisfying. These usually become gradually less frequent with age, or if their relationships deteriorate. After the first adulterous experience, it is very easy for extramarital episodes to become a habit. Actions lead to habits, but it is never too late to change or to break a habit.

It seems to me then that for both men and women, whereas regular sexual activity is not absolutely essential for the body's healthy functioning, it does seem to be an important ingredient in the emotional and psychological well-being of those who have become accustomed to it. Conversely, let us not overlook the opposite consideration of the role of physical fitness in sexuality. The healthy and fit person almost always enjoys an increased ability to perform sexually, for which reason it is preferable for husbands and wives to participate jointly in their exercise programs (*see* chapter thirteen). For the single person, there is no doubt that a strong, fit body is not only more attractive to the opposite sex, but also bestows on the owner much-enhanced self-confidence in all interpersonal relationships with others of either sex.

In conclusion then, it seems that the celibate can do without sexual activity. The profligate apparently cannot, at least, unless and until he decides he wants to change his habit patterns. Paul said: "But if they cannot contain, let them marry: for it is better to marry than to burn" (1 Corinthians 7:9). But if, for any reason, marriage is not possible for the Christian single adult, since there is not any very effective fire extinguisher to quench the burning, he or she can, at the very least, through both sublimation and prayer, somewhat control the supply of inflammable fuel!

12

Fat or Fit

WE HAVE THOUGHT through several destructive habits and have considered the importance of caring for many physical needs in our quest for bodily health. Now we come to the two most common problem areas which are closely related to one another and which are also, for many people, both the most important and the most difficult to deal with. They are the control of body weight and the maintaining of cardiovascular-pulmonary (heart, blood vessels, and lung) fitness through adequate exercise.

I heard recently of a pastor who greatly desired to move to a large church in a wealthy suburb. He was favorably interviewed by the pulpit committee and preached an excellent sermon to the congregation. Yet he was turned down. Several months later, he happened to meet a member of the committee and asked him why this had happened. To his dismay he was told that, since he was easily fifty pounds overweight, the committee had decided to reject him, because they felt that he was not living what he was preaching, that his manifest lack of self-discipline was at variance with scriptural principles of self-control and personal holiness, and that, as such, he was not a good witness for Christ.

Obesity is by far the commonest single sign of physical unfitness in America. It is the natural result of the combination of gluttony and physical inactivity and is most common in middle life. It is a grim predictor of serious

illness to come, and although being overweight per se is not potentially fatal, it is associated with a variety of medical conditions which do shorten life. For example, it is almost always a common denominator in most heart diseases, high blood pressure, arteriosclerosis, diabetes, gall-bladder disease, and shortness of breath. Obesity may actually result from certain disorders of metabolism, the endocrine glands, or the central nervous system, but these are all very rare.

Every extra pound of fat represents hundreds of extra feet of blood vessels your heart has to pump blood through. For every ten pounds overweight, an average adult can expect to die two years earlier than he otherwise would. That's a whole decade of lost life as the penalty for the uncontrolled eating that produces fifty pounds of ugly fat! Next to sex, eating is the most satisfying of life's pleasures, but overindulgence leads to inexorable destructive effects.

Consider some simple mathematics. One of God's natural laws is that of the conservation of energy. Every ounce of food you eat is potential energy. You must either burn this off with exercise, or it will be stored as fat. Unfortunately, excess calories don't just pass out in the urine. In one pound of fat, there are 3,500 calories. Eat one day, one week, or one month, 3,500 calories more than your body burns up, and you automatically gain a pound of weight. Conversely, eat that much less over any period of time, and you will lose a pound. If you eat only forty more calories per meal than your body needs, you will gain one pound per month, twelve pounds per year. To lose that much weight, you must either eat that 120 calories less per day than your body needs, or do 120 calories' worth of extra exercise. It is your choice, but the easiest is to do a bit of both: eat less and exercise more.

What did you weigh at eighteen, or in college, or, at the latest, at age twenty-five? Your full growth was then complete (nearer eighteen for women, nearer twenty-five for men), and *if you were in good health at that time*, your weight then is your ideal weight for the rest of your life. Any extra, now, is probably fat. However, even if your weight is the same now as then, unless you are taking plenty of exercise regularly, you will probably have lost muscle mass and replaced it with fat.

Gently pinch the skin and underlying fat at the back of the upper arm, a couple of inches below the armpit. More than an inch between your fingers indicates excessive fat. Better yet, your physician can do a test with special calipers such as the Lederle Skinfold Gauge which measures thickness of fat under the skin. Here is a sobering thought: The fat you can feel under your skin directly reflects the fat enveloping and choking your heart, and inexorably clogging your arterial blood supply. An even more accurate test, involving being weighed floating in water, can reveal the percentage of your body weight which is fat. Any of these tests can alert you if there is a need to reverse the trend of your sedentary routine by building up muscle mass with more exercise, and reducing fat by cutting down calorific (but not nutritional) intake. See Appendix B for weight charts.

If you want to lose weight, there is no shortage of reduction diets available in popular bookstores. There are also several Christian books out now, all essentially giving the message that being overweight is contrary to God's will and that spiritual resources can help you to reduce. Most of them, however, fail to stress that, whereas spiritual power is indeed available, we still have to appropriate it. We still need to use willpower, self-control, and self-discipline. Temperance is part of the Fruit of the Spirit (*see* Galatians 5:22, 23), but it seems unpopular with fat Christians, who prefer love, joy, peace, and so forth! It is curious that, whereas smoking and drinking alcohol are often so condemned in

Christian circles, overeating is condoned as not being so serious a sin, if one at all.

In general, to maintain good general nutrition without excess calories, the best diet should follow the suggestions in chapter nine. Then, to lose weight, simply reduce the quantities you are accustomed to. Not that easy, I know. So if you feel you need the help and discipline of a detailed, meal-by-meal diet, my best recommendations are the diets for obesity put out by the Mayo Clinic, Rochester, Minnesota. Ask for the 1,500-calorie diet if you are ten to thirty pounds overweight, the 1,200-calorie diet if over thirty pounds overweight. Check with your physician first before getting started, in case he might know if you have some individual contraindication.

Like smoking and drinking, eating to excess is learned behavior, and can, therefore, be unlearned. Motivation or incentive is an absolute prerequisite. You've got to *want* to eat less. Determination to persist is another essential ingredient for success. Making a list of good reasons to lose weight helps you to maintain progress. Make your own list. It might include some of these:

1. *Aesthetics*—you look better and appear more attractive if you're not fat.
2. *Economics*—junk foods are costly in comparison with their nutritional value.
3. *Example to your children*—whose attitudes and beliefs about food are learned from their parents.
4. *Self-mastery*—are you controlling or being controlled?
5. *Health*—your knowledge of the medical dangers of obesity.
6. *Well-being*—you feel physically so much better when you're not overweight.
7. *God's will for your life*—do you want to live for

Him? If so, fat or fit? Remember, your body is His temple.

Let your attitude be positive and self-reinforcing. Don't think of dieting as a deprivation of pleasure, but rather the positive achievement of a better self-image, a personality capable of discipline and mastery, and a Christian living victoriously for God.

What learned behavior stimulates you to eat? Is it your cultural habits inherited or absorbed from your parents or from peers or from advertising? Or is it the sight or smell of food, a vending machine, the time of day, or some emotional upset? Try to distinguish in yourself between stimulation of the appetite and actual hunger. We all so often eat when we are not really hungry. We often just crave something in the mouth—food, drink, chewing gum, or a cigarette. Freud called it oral regression. That's just about it, so often, just infantile thumb-sucking—regressing back to the comfort, the satisfaction, and the sense of security of something, anything, in the mouth!

If you're "for real" and genuinely want to reduce, here are some rules for losing weight you might consider imposing on yourself:

1. Don't try crash or fad diets. They are almost always deficient in vitamins and minerals. Especially dangerous to health are very low-calorie/high-protein liquid preparations. Several deaths from heart failure have been reported from their use. You'll lose weight all right on these diets, but you'll quickly get bored with their lack of variety. Then when you quit the diet, you'll gain the weight right back. This seesawing of weight puts a great strain on your cardiovascular system. Better it is to eat a fully nutritious, balanced diet, but one smaller in quantities. Avoid foods labeled *dietetic*. They usually contain mannitol or sorbitol, artificial sweeteners for use by diabetics, not dieters.

2. Eat slowly. This allows time for the stomach to stretch, a process which takes several minutes and which signals that enough food has been taken in. If you eat too rapidly, the feeling of satiety, or fullness, may not come until fully ten minutes after you've eaten enough. During that ten minutes, you are still feeling hungry and therefore still eating and thereby absorbing more food than you need. Discipline yourself to stop eating when you know you have had enough, even though you are still feeling slightly hungry. Ten minutes later, your stomach will have stretched, and the feeling of hunger will have gone. A glass of water before the meal will help you reach that full feeling more quickly. Allow at least twenty to thirty minutes for each meal.

3. Reread the suggestions in chapter nine on what to eat at mealtimes to maintain balanced nutrition without getting fat. If you are already fat, you still need a good protein and whole-grain-cereal breakfast each morning to build up the blood-sugar level gradually for the day's work. If you make this the largest meal of the day, it will reduce the craving for a junk-food snack at midmorning, and you will have all day to burn off the calories with the day's activities.

4. It is especially important for overweight people to go for a high-fiber lunch like a small chef's salad, or one with bulk vegetables such as lettuce, spinach, celery, carrots, or radishes with cottage cheese and fresh fruit. These have the double benefit of producing a sensation of fullness without giving very many calories and also giving the roughage necessary for healthy functioning of the lower bowel. Resist a midafternoon snack.

5. Complete your daily nutritional needs with a small, well-balanced dinner of cooked meat and vegetables, supplemented with vitamin and mineral tablets. Have this meal as early in the evening as practical, not just before going to bed. Remember, all quantities must be small. Again, no snack at bedtime.

6. Eat less fat and more fiber. Remove visible fat from meat. Go for poultry and fish more often. Bake or broil rather than fry. Use skim milk and polyunsaturated margarine, and, of course, absolutely eliminate all junk food. Don't even keep what you know to be junk food in the house. Take only whole-grain cereals and breads. Learn to enjoy raw, high-fiber fruits, vegetables, and seeds.

7. If you feel you have to succumb to a between-meals snack, try a drink of water first. If that doesn't help, take some bouillon, tomato juice, or a couple of raw carrots, celery, or an apple—but *no junk!*

8. Weigh yourself naked once each week, at the same time, on the same scale. How about every Sunday morning, before you go off to church? You might have something very tangible to thank and praise the Lord for! Be content with losing one pound per week. If you don't try to rush it, you are more likely to maintain the progress. Be patient and you will be more successful in the long run.

9. An occasional one-day fast, whether or not you are overweight, can sometimes be a good thing. It will shrink your stomach so that the next day a smaller meal will seem enough. Many who fast frequently claim that it "purifies the system," whatever that may mean. It obviously does reduce the work load on the liver and kidneys for several hours, thereby enabling them to catch up on any backlog of overdue metabolism or excretion. There are many references in the Bible to fasting, usually in association with some spiritual discipline or prayer. However, never fast for more than three days without medical surveillance. Once the liver's store of glycogen is burned up, significant biochemical changes take place, which can lead to a high mood, loss of contact with reality, and eventually to hallucinations. Spiritual ecstasy during a period of prayer and fasting is sometimes heightened by this chemically induced euphoria.

10. Fasting for long periods to lose large amounts of

weight rapidly is medically sound, so long as protein and vitamin supplements are taken, together with adequate fluids, which would avoid the biochemical problems. This drastic and very thorough method *must,* however, only be done under a physician's supervision, preferably in a hospital. Long-term, unsupervised fasting, or serious undereating, occasionally attempted by adolescent girls who are often schizophrenic or obsessed with body-image problems, leads to a very dangerous condition known as anorexia nervosa. This disease, the opposite of obesity, can lead to death from starvation or secondary infection and is in urgent need of both medical and psychiatric treatment.

11. If you cannot be successful on your own, don't be too proud to seek help and support. Join the local group of Overeaters Anonymous or Weight Watchers in your area. They both can provide much-needed group support to the struggling individual. Ask your physician for a prescribed diet if you feel you need something more than simply disciplining yourself to eat less. Discuss your weight problem and your efforts to combat it, with a small, select group of friends who are perhaps in a similar situation. Mutual encouragement can help a lot.

12. Do not take appetite-suppressant medications for more than two to three weeks. After this, continuing use will probably no longer reduce appetite, and weight lost on them will be gained right back. Also, the amphetamines most of them contain, while elevating the depressed mood of starting dieters, can cause addiction.

13. Treat the cause, not just the resulting symptoms. Obesity is only a result; overeating and underexercising are its causes. Consider why you overeat. For many there are complicated personal or emotional problems that can lead to it. A brief course of individual psychotherapy from an experienced, sympathetic, and supportive family physician or psychiatrist can often get to the root of the matter. Seriously, try some counseling.

You will be surprised at how much it can help you to understand yourself, your problem, and how best to deal with it. Remember to think positively. Weight control should not be thought of as suffering or some painful self-denial, but rather as a means of boosting one's sense of self-esteem and gaining self-mastery.

14. If you want to count calories and work everything out mathematically, get yourself any little booklet which tells you exactly how many calories there are in commonly consumed foods and drinks. Then aim to eat daily just ten calories per pound of your desired weight. For example, if you want to get down to 130 pounds, eat only 1,300 calories per day. Again, consult your family doctor for details about this.

15. Plan your diet thoughtfully and sensibly. Plan each menu carefully. The diet must be nutritious, yet not high in calories. It must be easy to follow and easy to integrate into your normal daily routine. It need not be either elaborate or expensive. Go grocery shopping only when necessary. Prepare a list and stick to it. Don't shop when you're feeling hungry.

16. Finally, exercise is essential to burn off as many calories as possible. But you *must* work up *gradually,* preferably under your doctor's scrutiny. Don't do too much at once if you are not used to it. You might drop dead from a heart attack. Progress slowly.

I guarantee to you, from both professional knowledge and personal experience, that the appropriate combination of disciplined dietary intake and sensibly escalated exercise, assures anyone, not only of weight control immediately, but also eventually of excellent physical conditioning and well-being.

How to achieve a good exercise program is the subject of the rest of this book.

13

Exercise: Fun, Not Pain

WHAT YOU ARE about to read could add ten or more years to your earthly life, if you desire that enough to apply these concepts and actions to yourself. With the exception of being inflicted with cancer or a few other relatively rare conditions, a body that is in a good state of physical fitness can resist and postpone death from many causes for a long time. Certainly death from most diseases associated with the heart, blood vessels, or lungs can be staved off for many years. Even if you don't desire to live longer, the quality of your life, long or short, will be greatly enhanced by exercising to fitness.

Front-page headlines in the *New York Times* reported on November 28, 1977, from Miami Beach: "Study of 17,000 Men Indicates Vigorous Sports Protects Heart." The occasion was the annual convention of the American Heart Association. Finally, what had been suspected for years had been proven by documented statistics on death and disease. These were compiled over a ten-year period from records of thousands of men involved in all levels of physical activity, from the completely sedentary to the athlete. The study showed that these men, all Harvard alumni, had had fewer heart attacks the more active they had been, and that strenuous, regular, leisure-time physical exertion produced a "definite protective effect." These principles are equally true for women.

Of particular interest was the finding that small amounts of activity required in "light" sports, such as bowling, baseball, golf, and so forth, which require little energy output, had no protective effect. On the other hand, those men who were regularly involved in brisk walking, climbing stairs, jogging, swimming, tennis, squash, or handball had far lower incidences of both fatal and nonfatal heart attacks. It seems that a minimum of three hours per week, with the expenditure of 2,000 calories each week, was the level to aim for. Those alumni who expended fewer than 2,000 calories per week (300 per day) above their normal daily routine had a 64 percent higher risk of heart attack than their more energetic classmates.

Also put to rest in the study was the oft-heard opinion that those who are able to exercise strenuously are those who are more fit or more athletic to begin with. The exact opposite was discovered. Men who had been athletes while at Harvard were not protected in later years if they had failed to remain physically active. Conversely, men who had not been athletes in college had a reduced risk of heart disease if they had started exercising after graduating. Most gratifying of all was the finding that the protective effect of exercise was even of significance in men who had such high-risk factors as high blood pressure, overweight, cigarette smoking, previous inactivity, and family history of heart disease.

Why is it that regular exercise is so protective? The basic answer is that rhythmic and vigorous contraction and relaxation of the muscles and heart (also a muscle) during a long enough period of time lead to increases in their blood supply. Both the size and the number of blood vessels over a period of time are increased as a result of regular activity. In the case of the heart, the increase in the internal diameter of the coronary artery and its branches reduces the likelihood of a heart attack occurring. Also, the increased number of these branches significantly improves chances of recovery if an attack should strike.

Also increased during exercise are body temperature, heart and respiration rates, oxygen consumption and sweating. All these physiological effects lead in turn to these well-recognized signs of physical fitness:

1. Better cardiovascular efficiency
2. Lower blood pressure
3. Lower serum cholesterol and triglycerides
4. Higher ratio of high-density lipoproteins
5. Increased coronary circulation
6. Reduction of excess body fat
7. Increased muscle size and strength (enabling the heart, for example, to pump more blood per beat)
8. Increased ability to consume oxygen

Exercise physiologists can measure oxygen consumption by collecting and analyzing the expired air of someone walking or jogging on a treadmill. Between 40 and 50 milliliters of oxygen consumed per kilogram of body weight indicates good to excellent conditioning. Below 40 indicates poor shape, above 60 is found in the superathlete. If you can run one and one half miles in twelve minutes, this would mean an oxygen consumption of 42 milliliters per kilogram, which is fairly good conditioning. If you can do one and three quarter miles in twelve minutes, you will have consumed just over 50 milliliters per kilogram, which means you are in very good shape.

Now for ourselves, before we even start an exercise or get-fit program, we need to evaluate how unfit we are, because the worse shape we're in, the lower the level of activity must be at the start, and the slower must be the initial rate of progress. Too much too quickly could be dangerous.

First, if you are over thirty-five, have a physical examination which should include a stress EKG (*see* Appendix A). This test will pick up as many as 95 percent of patients with coronary-artery disease, or the imminent potential for a heart attack, as contrasted with only 15 percent using a resting EKG. Then, if your doctor says your heart and general condition are okay, try, over a few weeks, to build up from walking to jogging, gradually increasing the distance and pace. Increase slowly. Slow down or stop when you get out of breath or if you feel any ache or pain across the front of your chest. This pain is called angina and indicates too much load on the heart.

When you feel ready, take a stopwatch with you to a measured track at your local high school, YMCA, or YWCA. See how far you can walk/jog/run in twelve minutes. This simple test which you can give yourself was developed by Dr. Kenneth Cooper of Dallas, Texas, a leading authority on exercise physiology. To avoid over-exertion, try the talk test. Go with someone while you jog. If shortness of breath prevents conversation while you are running, slow down, you're overdoing it. Don't be impatient. Getting fit takes several weeks, with gradual escalation of pace and distance. Stop at once if you have any pain in the chest.

If you are under fifty years of age, you should be able to cover one and one half miles in those twelve minutes, if you're in reasonable shape. Men over fifty should be able to do one and one quarter miles; women under thirty, one and one third miles; over thirty, one and one fifth miles in twelve minutes.

Another very simple test of fitness is the measurement of resting pulse rates. Resting means having been totally relaxed for at least fifteen to twenty minutes. The average unfit American has a resting heart rate of 72 beats per minute in males, up to 80 in women. A male with a pulse over 80 is in poor shape; for women, over 85 is also poor. By contrast, in response to a good conditioning program the heart will enlarge and increase its volume of blood pumped per beat. This will reduce the number of beats needed to circulate the blood. A man or woman in excellent shape can expect the rate to drop into the 50s or even 40s. Mine is in the 40s; many top athletes' pulses are in the 30s.

Studies done at Northwestern University on 1,300 men revealed three times as many sudden deaths in those with resting heart rates of over 90 as in those with rates under 70. Another measure of fitness is that of the ability of the heart rate to return to less then 100 within ten minutes of severe exercise. This is the medical definition of being in good shape.

If you are only fifteen pounds overweight, your heart may have to beat up to ten times more per minute. If you smoke twenty cigarettes per day as well, or if you are thirty to fifty pounds overweight, your heart rate may be increased by as much as twenty extra beats per minute. That's almost thirty thousand more beats per day, over 10 million extra beats per year. No wonder life expectancy is reduced!

Once you've tested yourself and discovered how fit or unfit you are, what about creating a weekly program for yourself? Not everyone enjoys walking or jogging. Many prefer bicycling, swimming, or some competitive ball game (individual, not team). Although daily participation in a sport is ideal, three nonconsecutive days each week is a good second best for frequency. As little as three consecutive days of immobility can lead to significant loss of muscle mass and strength.

Let us now consider various types of exercise and see how effective they are in serving such purposes as building muscle tone and strength, improving flexibility, helping in weight loss, relieving emotional tension, and getting one's heart and lungs in good condition. There are four basic types of exercise: isometrics, isotonics, anaerobics, and aerobics.

1. *Isometrics* ("equal measure") consist of contracting muscles without producing movement. Usually one set

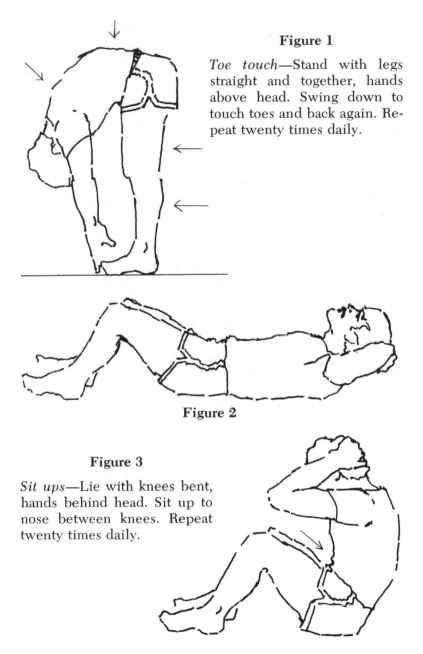

Figure 1

Toe touch—Stand with legs straight and together, hands above head. Swing down to touch toes and back again. Repeat twenty times daily.

Figure 2

Figure 3

Sit ups—Lie with knees bent, hands behind head. Sit up to nose between knees. Repeat twenty times daily.

of muscles is tensed, either against another set or against an immovable object or piece of apparatus. Six seconds at a time at full or almost-full strength is recommended by experts. If this is done two or three times daily over a period of several weeks, it will increase the size and strength of the large skeletal muscles of the arms, legs, back, and abdomen. Isometric exercises are useful in bedridden patients and in astronauts in space to prevent atrophy (wasting) of muscles through inactivity.

The best of the isometrics is the gut exercise which can be done sitting erect in a chair, even at work in the office. Draw in your abdominal muscles as far and as hard as you can and hold it for six seconds. Done several times daily, this is guaranteed to get rid of your potbelly and reduce your waist measurement. Arm wrestling is good for the ego if you win, but it's good for little else.

Isometrics build a beautiful body which the opposite sex will admire at the beach, but they are useless for general conditioning, since they do nothing to improve the heart, lungs, or circulatory system. It's rather like giving your car a fresh coat of paint when it really needs a new engine. ". . . for the Lord seeth not as man seeth; for man looketh on the outward appearance, but the Lord looketh on the heart" (1 Samuel 16:7). Also, a word of caution: Isometric exercises greatly increase blood pressure during contraction. These could be dangerous to susceptible people, because they could cause a stroke, and therefore they should not be practiced by elderly people.

2. *Isotonics* ("equal tension") are exercises which contract muscles and produce movement. Like isometrics, they are no good in themselves for building up efficiency and endurance in heart and lungs, but have merit in keeping muscles and joints strong and supple. Weight lifting, bowling, and calisthenics are the best examples. Weight lifting, as with isometrics, builds big muscles to an unnatural degree, but calisthenics are better in that

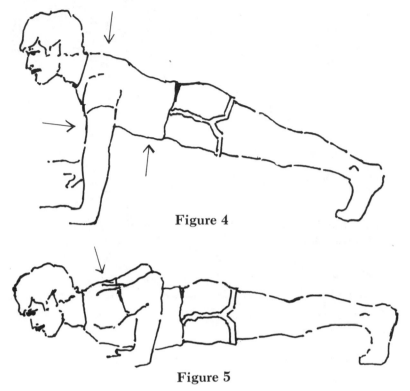

Figure 4

Figure 5

Push ups—Prone position, legs and arms straight. Bend arms to nose touching floor and push back up again. Repeat twenty times daily.

they develop muscles along the natural body lines, slimming you where you need it and building up deficient areas.

Touching your toes, sit-ups, and push-ups are the best three, and doing twenty to thirty of each a couple of times daily will keep your back and abdominal muscles particularly in good shape. (*See* diagrams.) Many other floor or mat exercises are good for maintaining suppleness and agility in the joints, and flexibility and tone in the major muscle groups.

A special type of activity I highly recommend to all

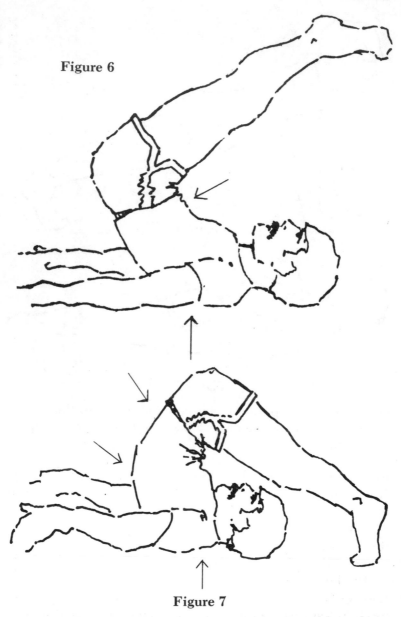

Figure 6

Figure 7

Full inversion—Flat on back, arms by side. Lift legs together over head and touch floor behind. Repeat twenty times daily.

Figure 8

Calf stretch—Stand, as shown, at arm's length from wall. Bend arms till nose touches wall. Keep back heel on ground. Hold ten seconds. Repeat with legs reversed. Repeat five times daily.

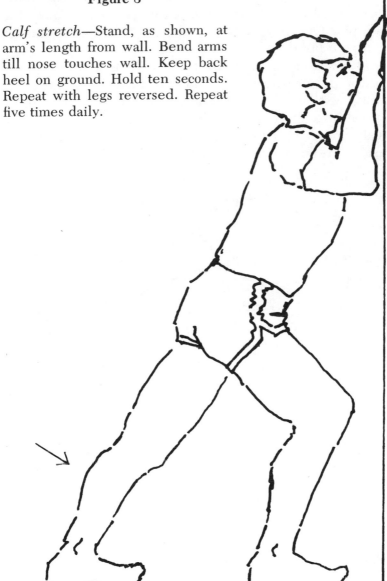

desiring strong, supple bodies are the relatively recently developed series of stretching exercises, essential for the competitive athlete, but beneficial to all. (*See* the accompanying diagrams for details.)

These exercises and stretches will develop for you a better posture in sitting and standing. They will help slim most fat areas, and keep joints and muscles supple and strong. You will become able to breathe better and to walk properly, without slouching. Your physical attitude usually reflects your mental and spiritual attitudes.

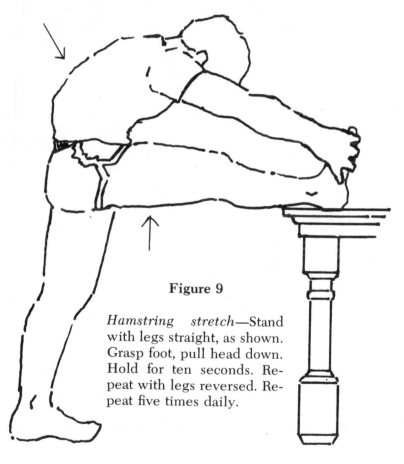

Figure 9

Hamstring stretch—Stand with legs straight, as shown. Grasp foot, pull head down. Hold for ten seconds. Repeat with legs reversed. Repeat five times daily.

3. *Anaerobics* ("without oxygen") are forms of exertion that are either too short in duration to have any conditioning benefit or training effect, or so violent that a huge "oxygen debt" is rapidly built up, and you are forced to stop very soon. For example, running for a bus or walking a couple of blocks to the nearest mailbox doesn't last long enough to be of any benefit. Oxygen-

Figure 10

Hip and thigh slimmer—Especially good for women. Sit as shown grasping foot with hand. Twist hips. Hold ten seconds. Repeat other side. Repeat five times daily.

debt exercises are such activities as windsprints, interval training, the hundred-yard dash, swimming a couple of fast lengths, or a one-quarter-mile bicycle sprint.

These are all good for the competitive athlete to build up the stamina and speed needed to put him ahead of his opponent, but they are of no value in improving the general condition of the body, because they last too short a time. They are only of value to the athlete if he is already in great shape. If he is not, they could kill him! They have no place in a fitness training program for the unfit person, because they are of too short duration and could even cause a heart attack.

4. *Aerobics* ("with oxygen"). Oxygen is the key to life, and the key to full fitness and health is the body's ability to deliver more oxygen to all its cells and tissues. Deprived of oxygen for even three minutes, the body dies, or at least suffers irreversible brain damage. The problem is that even though the body can store food (as fat), it

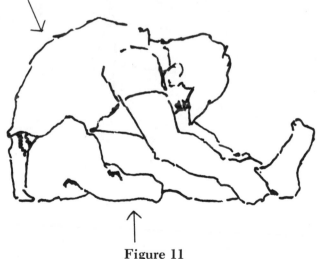

Figure 11

Back and leg stretch—Sit, as shown, with one sole flat against inside of opposite knee. Grasp ankle, pull head down. Hold ten seconds. Repeat other side. Repeat five times daily.

cannot store oxygen with which that food is burned to provide needed energy. Therefore, the oxygen supply has to be coming in and the waste product carbon dioxide has to be going out all the time. The faster the body can deliver oxygen from the air to its inner, remotest parts, the fitter that body becomes. What is the delivery system? It is comprised of the lungs, heart, blood vessels, and blood. Exercises, therefore, that develop maximum efficiency in these organs are the ones called aerobics, and they are the ones essential both to get you and keep you in great shape. An additional ben-

Figure 12

Adductor stretch—Sit, as shown, with left leg straight, left hand holding right foot over left knee, right arm resting on right knee. Hold ten seconds. Repeat other side. Repeat five times daily.

efit these exercises confer is the tendency to decrease rather than increase appetite.

What are the aerobic exercises? The best by far is running, followed by bicycling, swimming, running in place, skipping rope, playing basketball, singles squash, handball, badminton, and tennis, in about that order. (With the sole exception of basketball, team sports are virtually impossible to evaluate, both because the energy expenditure can be so different among team members and also because such a variable percentage of the time is spent standing around or sitting out the game.) However, all of these activities are of no value unless done for sufficiently long a time to produce a training effect.

How long is sufficiently long?

Those really interested in this should get the little paperback *Aerobics,* by Kenneth H. Cooper. It might be the best dollar or so you ever invested. Here is a brief summary of Dr. Cooper's main points.

He states that if exercise is vigorous enough to produce a sustained heart rate of 150 beats per minute or more, the training-effect benefits begin about five minutes after the exercise starts and continues as long as the exercise is performed. Sufficiently long, therefore, cannot be less than five minutes.

Doctor Cooper has developed a very interesting point system which enables anyone seriously wanting to get fit to follow a program for himself. To achieve thirty points every week would get you fit, and then keep you fit. (A goal of fifty points per week, however, is more appropriate for those in their teens and twenties.)

He recommends for the average person, male or female, five points per day for six days each week, or ten points on each of three nonconsecutive days.

Five points are earned by walking two and one half miles in under thirty-six minutes, running one mile in less than eight minutes, or by swimming 600 yards in less than fifteen minutes, by cycling five miles in less than twenty minutes, running in place or skipping rope for thirteen minutes, or by playing squash, basketball, racquetball, badminton, or handball for thirty-five minutes continuously. (Standing around time doesn't count.) Any one of these should be done six days out of seven. (*See* Appendix I.)

On the basis of only three outings per week, you need to double these performances to earn ten points each time. Ten points could be earned by walking five miles in less than one hour and twelve minutes, running two miles in under sixteen minutes, swimming twelve hundred yards in under half an hour, cycling ten miles in forty minutes, skipping or stationary running for twenty-six minutes (terribly boring!) or playing squash or another active sport for one hour and ten minutes (a lot more fun). These figures, by the way, are far from arbitrary. Doctor Cooper has done thousands of man-hours of research, mainly on U.S. Air Force personnel, and he is able to back up his results, and therefore his recommendations, with hundreds of irrefutable statistics.

These kinds of exercises, incidentally, not only burn up calories while they are being performed. For as much as four hours after stopping exercising, the body continues to burn calories at a higher rate than in the sedentary person. If you are not so much interested in the aerobic points system, but are more concerned with burning up calories, see Appendixes J and K on the calorific expenditures of various activities and Appendix L on contraindications to strenuous exercise.

As stated earlier, the easiest form of regular aerobic exercise we all can take is walking. It is only a step up from that to jogging and running. I am so convinced that all Christians should do one of these three that I want to devote a separate chapter to it. To me, this next chapter is the message of this book. All the rest has been introduction!

14

Walk, Jog, Run

ALMOST ALL OF US can walk, though so often in our mechanized and rushed society some of us try to do it as little as possible. However, I'm not so much concerned at this point about the need to use your feet instead of your car for short trips. I have already stressed this. I am concerned here about the use of walking and jogging as a planned activity which could become a part of your daily routine and life-style. This is to be specifically for the purpose of helping you to lose or control weight and to give you a healthy level of fitness, especially in your heart and lungs.

According to Dr. Cooper's point system (*see* chapter 13), a good level of fitness can be achieved by earning thirty points per week. Translated into walking, this means we should strive to walk two and one half miles six out of seven days every week, or five miles, on three nonconsecutive days, weekly. This should be at a good, brisk pace, not just an idle stroll, and represents a total time investment of between three and three and one half hours per week, depending on your pace.

That still leaves 165 hours in the week for all your other responsibilities, including work, leisure, and sleep. I submit that since this investment is less than 2 percent of your total time available, it is a pretty good one, if it gives you ten extra years of life, to say nothing of the quality of those years, quite apart from their duration. It is never easy to find time. We have to *make* time. It is a matter of priorities. If you want to do something badly enough, you will budget the time for it in advance.

First thing in the morning is probably the least disruptive to one's normal routine. Many claim that it is the most exhilarating; the fresh bracing air at its least polluted, the sparkling dew of dawn welcoming the sunrise, virtually deserted roads. The lunch hour is my personal preference because, being self-employed, I can take off as long as I need. After work and before the evening meal is probably the most popular, but you must be sure you are clearly visible after dark. Wear white clothing or some reflective tape, and walk or run on the left of the road facing oncoming traffic.

Quite frankly, admitting this to be a bit of a tough attitude, I feel conversely that if you are *not* willing to make this time investment to take care of God's temple, you don't deserve to live out a long life free of some discomfort in your declining years. At least this book is making the point that much of that suffering is avoidable.

Walking, of course, can be done in ordinary clothes, and unless your pace is very brisk, you would not necessarily sweat much or feel the need for a bath or shower afterwards. However, if you do take up this challenge and start walking regularly, it would be better to get into tennis shorts, shirt, and sneakers, with a covering sweater and a pair of old, long pants for colder weather. There are two reasons for this: First, if you are not in your ordinary clothes, you will be more willing to step up the pace and not be bothered if you start sweating. Second, it makes it very easy to progress to jogging when you have been walking long enough to know you can do it for a short distance without danger to your heart.

Assuming you have now progressed to being able to walk your two and one half miles in thirty-six minutes or less, you are now ready to start jogging. Jogging, by the way, merely means running at a fairly slow, comfortable pace, not worried about speed or racing against others or a clock. In any case, distance is far more important than speed. You may remember from elementary physics that to move a given weight a given distance requires almost the same amount of energy, whether it is moved quickly or slowly. The body is similar. You expend only slightly more energy running a mile than you do walking it (15 to 30 percent, depending on speed). However, since you can go twice the distance in your time available by running, you can thereby double the energy and calories used up and also obtain increased cardiovascular benefits. So jogging is better than walking, but walking is better than sitting!

In England, during the war, I was a Boy Scout patrol leader, and, on our many camping trips out in the peaceful countryside, we would travel with all our tents and other equipment at "Scouts' pace." This consisted of walking and jogging alternately, two and one half minutes of each. By this means we were easily able to cover five miles every hour. Even as ten- to twelve-year olds, we constantly amazed ourselves at what large distances we were able to cover with such relatively little effort. At the day's end we were never exhausted, just happily tired.

Now, almost forty years later, I still enjoy jogging and walking along the tree-lined country roads of Fairfield County, Connecticut. You can do the same, if you want to, and enjoy the exhilaration of the fresh air stimulating your lungs and the road flashing by under your feet. It is like a spiritual experience, a communing with creation, a feeling of oneness between your body and the beauties of nature, a special type of closeness to God.

Jogging doesn't have to be painful, indeed, it shouldn't be. Go at your own pace. When you get pooped, slow down to a walk. Soon you'll get your breath

Learning John's Gospel while jogging in my Medical Joggers'
T-shirt.

back, and you can start jogging again. If you try to do this a minimum of three times each week, you will be amazed at how soon you will be able to go distances you never imagined you could.

The secret is to work up both distance and pace gradually, and of these two, distance is by far the more important. Pace is only important if you are training for a race. You and I are not so much interested in becoming competitive athletes as becoming physically fit. *Long Slow Distance* is the secret, a better kind of LSD than the drug of that name.

Let me now share my own enthusiasm for running with you. Although I was on my prep school's cross-country running team, I never won a race, then or since, except a couple of sprints. After leaving school, I did not run again for twenty years, an experience which many reading this have shared. I did, however, during those years, play squash three or four times every week, which kept me in fairly reasonable (but not great) shape.

By my late thirties, I began to have a weight problem, and, realizing that squash alone was not enough, I started running a couple of times each week, my usual distances being either two or three miles, normally averaging six and one half minutes per mile. I gradually lost fifteen pounds, going from 195 down to 180 pounds, and felt a lot better. But there I stopped. I couldn't seem to lose any more. However, for a few years I was satisfied, maintaining 180 with my regular and enjoyable squash and short-distance-running program.

Then I began running with friends during the lunch hour in Central Park. We would go up the Park Drive West, facing the traffic, and then across to the reservoir. The track round the reservoir is 1.58 miles, and the number of times we went round depended on how we felt that day. Then back down the East Drive to Fifty-ninth Street for a shower and a ginger ale.

It was a subversive experience. I became hooked. The exhilaration of running at slower speed but longer distance, and the euphoric sense of achievement afterwards was a "high" no drug can match. As I gradually increased my distance, my weight started coming down again, and the more pounds I lost, the better I felt. (Today I am down to 169 pounds and still losing. Running LSD regularly, I can eat all I want and not gain!)

Then something most unexpected happened. Two of my Central Park friends, both older than I, successfully completed the New York City Marathon, and told me they were sure I could do the same. I was really shocked. The thought of my running 26.2 miles boggled my mind, but I accepted it as a personal challenge. At the time of this writing, I haven't done it yet, but I have run a twenty-five-mile fund-raising event, with only minor stiffness the next day. I am struggling, as you are.

In addition to lunch-hour outings in the city, I also run on weekends near my home in Connecticut. Although I go occasionally to the local high-school track, I much prefer the quiet back roads of Darien, where traffic is light and my only troubles are snowballs from kids, quips and expletives from the locals, and hostility from aggressive, noisy dogs defending their territory as I go trotting past.

Jogging is not painful if you build up the distance a little bit at a time. I started my training with just five miles, then over a period of three months built it up to seven and one half, ten, twelve and one half, then fifteen miles. Fifteen miles takes me a fraction over two hours, averaging about eight minutes per mile, a comfortable pace for a middle-aged man. It is a humbling thought, though, that as the next marathon winner is finishing, I will still have ten miles to go! But I'm told that in the marathon, winning is not so much getting there first, but just getting there!

I'm not, of course, saying that in order to keep the temple fit for God that all Christians should become marathon runners. We do need some measure of commitment, though, and a willingness to invest a little time and very little money. The only money investment I recommend is in a good pair of running shoes. Do be willing to spend twenty to thirty dollars on these. They are much better than regular sneakers in supporting your feet and protecting you from various pulled muscles, and so forth. All other jogging clothing can be old or cheap.

Time investment for the jogger is also minimal. It is the best value of any easily accessible exercise in terms of benefit gained in the time spent. Three one-half-hour outings (approximately three miles each time) each week will get you and keep you in very good shape. And remember how much better you will feel and function. Believe me, it is more than worth it.

Jogging can be fun in groups—groups from a neighborhood, a local church, an extended family. The fellowship of doing things together encourages one to get out on days when you don't feel like it. If friends are waiting for you to get started, you'll be there rather than be thought a quitter, and on your own good days, you can encourage others who are not feeling so good. Mothers with young children should especially become involved in groups, so as to share and rotate baby-sitting duties.

One of the essential rules of running for fitness is, "Train, don't strain!" In other words, don't overdo it in your enthusiasm. It will only sour you if you give yourself pain, and you will lose your desire to stick with it. Do what you can and then slow down or stop. You'll do better the next time out. The big lie of any sport is that it isn't any good unless it hurts. Running is, of course, a form of stress, but when applied in small doses, the body reacts by strengthening its defenses. Not only do you then become a better runner, but your increased strength helps defend you against many other stresses.

Remember from chapter ten that the body needs alternating periods of activity and rest. Don't, therefore, do two hard, long runs on consecutive days. For the beginner, it could be a short walk between two days of jogging a mile. For the marathon runner, it could be only ten miles between two days of fifteen or twenty miles! Find your own level. Remember also that running tends to tighten the calf and hamstring muscles, so don't forget to stretch them, as recommended in chapter thirteen, when you come in from your run.

It is not within the scope of this book to elaborate on the scores of technical and important details about running, which can greatly help the beginner. If, coming now toward the end of this book, you feel an urge to start exercising, I strongly encourage you, the beginning jogger, to beg, borrow, buy, or steal (temporarily only, of course) these three excellent books. (You will thoroughly enjoy them and be inspired by them.) They are: *Jog, Run, Race* by Joe Henderson; *Doctor Sheehan on Running* by George Sheehan; and *The Complete Book of Running* by James F. Fixx. (*See* Recommended Reading list for details.)

I am often asked what I think about when I'm running. I have two answers. First, I let my mind wander freely and enjoy the wide variety of thoughts that come in. It's like the free association of psychoanalysis. I like listening to my own thoughts. I like being alone occasionally. Life is usually so much talk, so many people—nice people, but talking people.

I wake up to the news on a clock-radio; my family chatters happily at breakfast; I read words and more words on the commuter train; my job consists all day of listening to people talking, complaining, arguing; and yet more words as I read to get myself to sleep at night.

But that break in the middle of the day is precious to

me. If it's an hour of squash, all my opponent and I say is the score as it progresses. The only other sound we hear is that of the ball meeting racket or wall. Running is even better. We don't talk much when we're going round the reservoir. Our friendship is based not on words, but on our shared activity. Running with others is better for the discipline of training. Running alone is better for personal recreation.

Running alone is not a lonely experience. I think and I look and I listen. I hear the birds, I see the squirrels, I hear the streams' rippling waters, and I see the trees and bushes changing colors with the seasons. And I think. I think about anything and everything that comes into my mind. I think through minor personal problems and often find answers while running. I also think about my body. I appreciate how it is feeling. I become more aware of its functioning. I develop a heightened sensitivity to its movements and revel in the satisfying pleasure of bounding with joy across the miles as I praise and thank God for my creation.

I also have a second answer to the question about thinking while running. Many times I memorize Scripture. I often carry with me, as I go, three-by-five cards with verses from the Bible written on them. I study them and repeat them over and over again as I run. I have found that I can learn about two verses per mile.

During the month of January, 1978, I ran seventy-nine miles and learned the entire Epistle of Paul to the Philippians. Now I'm into Colossians, and after that I hope to memorize the whole of John's Gospel, which will take me several months. Is it conceivable that in the years remaining to me I could memorize the whole of the New Testament? Possibly, but I probably started too late. But a young Christian could do it, if he caught the vision. It is doubly satisfying at the end of a two-hour outing, not only to have run fifteen miles, but also to have learned a chapter of the Bible by heart.

Remember that healthy mind in a healthy body? Get going, stick with it, and let these words of Paul inspire you as you go:

Know ye not that they which run in a race run all, but one receiveth the prize? So run that ye may obtain. And every man that striveth for the mastery is temperate in all things. Now they do it to obtain a corruptible crown; but we an incorruptible. I, therefore, so run, not as uncertainly; so fight I, not as one that beateth the air. But I keep under my body, and bring it into subjection . . . .

1 Corinthians 9:24–27

15

Press Toward the Mark

We have thought through a variety of self-destructive habits and have considered the problems of stress, sex, overweight, and the need for exercise. Our primary concern has been the responsibility of Christians to become and remain physically in excellent shape, so as to be maximally usable by God in His purposes for their lives. Jesus Christ is my King and your King. Let us get and stay fit for Him.

Writing to the Ephesians, Paul stated: ". . . no man ever yet hated his own flesh [body]; but nourisheth and cherisheth it . . ." (Ephesians 5:29). Was he kidding? In his day, certainly not; but today many Christians give the message to the world that his words are a farce. Countless Christians treat their bodies as if they do, in fact, hate them: They do not give them good (but not excessive) nutrition; and they do not take care of them by giving them their needed adequate bodily activity.

The powerful imagery of Ephesians 6:10–18 (look up and read this short passage), about the armor of God, is a colorful and challenging analogy to us with regard to our Christian responsibilities. One had to be physically fit and strong in those days to wear that heavy suit of full armor. We have to be fit similarly today to use effectively all those spiritual weapons, both defensive and offensive. I am totally convinced that God, in His wisdom and providence, has chosen to fashion us all in such a way that physical and mental fitness are, with very rare exceptions, necessary prerequisites to spiritual fitness. A healthy spirit usually occupies a healthy mind and body.

After I'd spoken on the subject of physical fitness at a meeting, a Christian came up to me afterwards and said, "Didn't Christ say, 'Take no thought for the body'?" Yes, in Matthew 6:25, in the Sermon on the Mount, He did indeed say that. But the context had to do with anxiety over the provision of the three basic essentials of life: food, raiment, and shelter. God obligates Himself to provide these to His children, and we, as believers, are encouraged to stop worrying about them. We are, however, responsible to worry about our poor bodily physical condition, and do something about it for the King's sake.

Paul was a very physical person in many ways. He had an acute understanding of the concept that his body was God's instrument, to be totally yielded to Him for the furtherance of His purposes. These purposes, unhappily, often involved pain and suffering: ". . . I bear in my body the marks of the Lord Jesus" (Galatians 6:17). In his letter to the Philippians, he expressed most forcefully his positive attitude and hope with respect to his physical life: ". . . that in nothing I shall be ashamed, but that with all boldness, as always, so now also Christ shall be magnified in my body, whether it be by life, or by death. For to me to live is Christ, and to die is gain" (Philippians 1:20, 21).

In his Second Letter to the Corinthians, Paul further emphasized the relationship between bodily actions and our destiny in Christ: "We are confident, I say, and willing rather to be absent from the body, and to be present with the Lord . . . . For we must all appear before the judgment seat of Christ; that every one may receive the things done in his body, according to that he hath done, whether it be good or bad" (2 Corinthians 5:8, 10). This should be a sobering thought to those Christians who are

"Lord knows what he's keeping in shape for *now*."
Drawing by Loreny; © 1977, The New Yorker Magazine, Inc.

going through this life neglecting or misusing their bodies, the instruments of God's service.

In the context of the needs of others, the apostle James warns us, in a verse applicable also to taking care of ourselves, that if ". . . ye give them not those things which are needful to the body; what doth it profit?" (James 2:16). Do you, do I, give to our bodies those things that are needful? Do we protect them from all harmful invasions? Do we provide them the best food in appropriate quantities? Do we give them the movements and the energy-burning activities they were created to perform?

The writer to the Hebrews exhorted them to ". . . lift up the hands which hang down, and the feeble knees; And make straight paths for your feet . . ." (Hebrews 12:12, 13). At the beginning of that same chapter, he said, ". . . let us lay aside every weight, and the sin which doth so easily beset us, and let us run with patience the race that is set before us, Looking unto Jesus the author and finisher of our faith . . ." (Hebrews 12: 1, 2). What could be a better verse of inspiration for the Christian dedicated to the commitment to lose weight and to exercise to fitness?

In conclusion, I want to leave with you a couple of verses I learned recently while jogging happily over slippery ice and snow, through freezing New England January winds: "Brethren, I count not myself to have apprehended [to be spiritually perfect]: but this one thing I do, forgetting those things which are behind, and reaching forth unto those things which are before, I press toward the mark for the prize of the high calling of God in Christ Jesus" (Philippians 3:13, 14).

Appendix A
Recommended Annual
Physical Examinations

IN ADDITION to the basic stethoscope-on-the-chest clinical evaluation, people over thirty-five should have several special tests done annually. An electrocardiogram (EKG), for example, done lying down is only useful for revealing a heart that is already damaged. Many a middle-aged man has had an EKG lying down and, after receiving reassurance of no abnormality, has dropped dead of a heart attack on leaving his doctor's office. A "stress" EKG, done while exercising, on the other hand, can much more readily reveal potential damage before it actually happens. Leads are attached to the chest of the patient while he is walking on a treadmill with a progressively increasing incline or pace; the heartbeats are displayed on an oscilloscope which is scrutinized by a doctor. An imminent coronary-artery block and most other cardiac abnormalities can be immediately visualized. If any such abnormality occurs, the treadmill is promptly stopped, a fatal heart stoppage is averted, and the patient is initiated into a treatment program to strengthen his heart and restore it to full health.

A useful blood test which can alert one to the danger of a heart attack is the measurement of high-density lipoproteins (HDLs). A strong inverse relationship exists between high-density lipoproteins and coronary heart disease (CHD), which means that decreased concentrations of HDL in plasma lead to an increased risk of CHD, whereas raised concentrations exert a protective effect.

A proctosigmoidoscopy (rectal examination with instrument) is also an annual must, especially for men over thirty-five. Thousands of very early cancers of the bowel or prostate have thereby been detected, long before the patient would have become aware of any symptoms, and swift surgery has averted death at far too early an age. The hemoccult slide test detects minute presence of blood in feces and represents a double check against intestinal cancer.

Other annual cancer detection tests for men should include chest X ray, GI series (X rays of esophagus, stomach, and upper intestine) and examination of urine for occult (unseen) blood.

For women over thirty-five an annual Papanicolaou (Pap test) for cervical cancer (of the uterus) and a thyroid-function test are essential for good preventive care. Women should examine their own breasts regularly and bring any lump or firm area to the attention of their doctors immediately. Breast cancer can occur rarely in men also. Although there are some reservations about the effect of X rays on the breast, a mammography should be done if any tumor is suspected, because the risk of failing to detect a cancer there then becomes greater than any possible damage that could be done by the radiation. All these tests can be lifesaving when pathology is discovered before symptoms are experienced, thereby giving early treatment a chance to prevent serious illness, or even death.

Special blood tests essential annually to all over thirty-five should include evaluations of cholesterol, triglycerides, and lipoprotein levels. These determine the status of fat metabolism with any consequent potential threat of arteriosclerosis, or narrowing of the blood vessels by fat-related deposits along their inner walls. Liver-function tests (transaminase, alkaline phosphatase, and bilirubin levels) are important year by year for all "social" drinkers to monitor and expose any unrecognized (or unconfessed!) increase in alcohol intake. Other blood chemistries should include measurements of sugar (*see* chapter eight and Appendix F), urea nitrogen (kidney function), uric acid (gout, arthritis, and so forth), and several others such as lactic dehydrogenase (LDH), albumin-globulin ratio, total protein, and concentrations of calcium, creatinine, and inorganic phosphates. A blood-serology test warns of any venereal disease.

A pulmonary (lung) function analysis is important for all smokers or people exposed to occupational or environmental breathing hazards. Again, early detection leading to change of habits or avoidance of further exposure can prevent serious problems later. Have your eyes and ears checked regularly too. Both vision and hearing can often decline imperceptibly and can many times be treated. Finally, don't forget your teeth. See your dentist regularly, every six months at least, for evaluation, treatment, and preventive care.

Appendix B
Weight Charts

DESIRABLE WEIGHTS in pounds for adult men and women, according to height and frame, in light (summer) indoor clothing with pockets empty and no shoes.

Men Aged Twenty-five and Over

Height	Small Frame	Medium Frame	Large Frame
5 1	112—120	118—129	126—141
5 2	115—123	121—133	129—144
5 3	118—126	124—136	132—148
5 4	121—129	127—139	135—152
5 5	123—133	130—143	138—156
5 6	128—137	134—147	142—161
5 7	132—141	138—152	147—166
5 8	136—145	142—156	151—170
5 9	140—150	146—160	155—174
5 10	144—154	150—165	159—179
5 11	148—158	154—170	164—184
6 0	152—162	158—175	168—189
6 1	156—167	162—180	173—194
6 2	160—171	167—185	178—199
6 3	164—175	172—190	182—204

Women Aged Twenty-five and Over

Height	Small Frame	Medium Frame	Large Frame
4 8	92— 98	96—107	104—119
4 9	94—101	98—110	106—122
4 10	96—104	101—113	109—125
4 11	99—107	104—116	112—128
5 0	102—110	107—119	115—131
5 1	105—113	110—122	118—134
5 2	108—116	113—126	121—138
5 3	111—119	116—130	125—142
5 4	114—123	120—135	129—146
5 5	118—127	124—139	133—150
5 6	122—131	128—143	137—154
5 7	126—135	132—147	141—158
5 8	130—140	136—151	145—163
5 9	134—144	140—155	149—168
5 10	138—148	144—159	153—173

Young people between eighteen and twenty-five years, subtract one pound for each year under twenty-five. Consult pediatrician's charts for adolescents and children.

For nude weight, deduct three pounds for men and two pounds for women.

Weight charts used by courtesy of the Metropolitan Insurance Company.

Appendix C
Mechanism of Action
of Marijuana

MOST DRUGS TAKEN REPEATEDLY lead to three related and progressive states within the user.

1. *Psychological dependence,* in which pleasurable or calming effects on the nervous system, produced by the drug,

    become necessary to maintain an optimal state of well-being
2. *Tolerance,* which is the need for increasing dosage to produce the required effect
3. *Physical dependence,* in which, because of an altered biochemical state, repeated doses have become necessary to prevent the discomfort of withdrawal symptoms

Located deep in the cerebrum (forebrain) are reflex centers recently discovered to be associated with the subjective sensations of pleasure. Stimulation of these pleasure centers by sensual drugs produces a psychological response in the brain, below a conscious level. This, in turn, adjusts the brain's internal controls so that discomfort results if the chemical is not supplied. The problem is that such unnatural, artificial stimulation of the pleasure centers eventually impairs their normal operation. A state of sensory deprivation then results, in which pleasurable responses actually become suppressed. Hence the tendency to take higher doses, leading to addiction.

Some have argued that a drug such as marijuana, which is not chemically addictive, but only psychologically addictive, is for that reason less dangerous, because it is considered to be more susceptible to rational control. In fact, however, because of the above-described mechanism of action, the two forms of addiction are so closely related as to make the argument false, because control or abstention becomes more than simply an act of the will. The late Dr. Hardin B. Jones of the University of California stated, "There is an inseparable relationship between chemical and psychological addiction, and the two forms coincide when the addictive substance is a pleasure-giving drug."

The problem with marijuana specifically is that its active ingredient, tetrahydrocannabinol (THC), is fat soluble and is, therefore, retained in the body for long periods (unlike water-soluble alcohol, which, if not stored as sugars or fat, is relatively quickly metabolized and excreted as carbon dioxide and water). Molecule for molecule, THC is ten thousand times more potent than alcohol in its ability to produce intoxication. Once dissolved, the THC is deposited in the fatty outer membranes of cells, including those in the brain, liver, and lungs, and on both red and white blood cells and sperm.

Postmortem specimens of brains of heavy users of marijuana reveal cerebral atrophy (shrinkage), the degree of which can be correlated with duration of use. This brain damage undoubtedly accounts for well-recognized behavioral changes in long-term pot smokers.

Genetic and embryologic damage has been shown in malformations in offspring of either male or female monkeys exposed to marijuana. In humans in the U.S.A. since the mid-1960s, when the use of pot increased greatly, there has been a parallel increase in birth defects in children of users, such as malformations of the hip joint and cardiovascular system. In the lungs, Swiss research has shown that marijuana smoke causes a greater degree of damage than tobacco smoke to lung cells, which eventually turn permanently from pink to black.

Physical effects of longtime use of marijuana include weight loss, wasting of muscles, loss of ability to enjoy any sensual pleasures, insomnia, irreversible brain damage, lowered resistance to infections, chromosome breakdown, genetic damage, emphysema and other related lung diseases, and sexual impotence and infertility. Recovery after cessation of longtime use takes months, or even years, and sometimes some of the damage done, such as in the brain or lungs, is permanent.

Suggested reference sources are:

Jones, Hardin B., "On the problems executives must anticipate with the growth of marijuana smoking." *Executive Health*, Vol. XIV, No. 1, October 1977. Published by and obtainable for $1.50 from Executive Health, P.O. Box 589, Rancho Santa Fe, California 02967.

Moore, Peter C., "What's wrong with marijuana?" *Monograph*, February 1978. Available for $1.00 from Focus Inc., 137 Red Fox Road, Stamford, Connecticut 06903.

Appendix D

Cancer's Seven Warning Signals
(From the American Cancer Society)

CAUTION

Change in bowel or bladder habits.
A sore that does not heal.
Unusual bleeding or discharge.
Thickening or lump in breast or elsewhere.
Indigestion or difficulty in swallowing.
Obvious change in wart or mole.
Nagging cough or hoarseness.

If YOU have a warning signal, see your doctor!

Appendix E

Effects of Excess
Refined Carbohydrates

WHITE GRANULATED SUGAR in its present retail form has only been around since about a hundred years ago, when the development of refining processes on a large scale eventually led to its becoming popular with the middle and lower classes. Previously it was found only as an expensive luxury, obtainable by the ounce from apothecaries, and most people of moderate means had to be content with raw honey for sweetening.

White sugar, or sucrose, is a disaccharide (double sugar) and is not natural to the body. It is refined from sugarcane or sugar beet. It has to be metabolized before it can be of any use, and this process breaks it down into fructose and glucose, both monosaccharides (single sugars). Fructose is found naturally in honey, fruits, and vegetables. Glucose (commercially sold as dextrose) is the natural sugar in the blood, which energizes all the body's cells. Other common sugars are lactose and galactose (in milk) and maltose (in malt).

Whereas fructose from fruit and so forth is a good, natural food, the body can handle it only in small quantities at a time. The major reason why refined sugar is so bad is that its immediate breakdown after absorption floods the system with too much fructose all at once. The liver can't handle the load, and many metabolic complications ensue. Most other starchy carbohydrates, such as flour or the glycogen stored in the liver, are polysaccharides (many sugars), and these also are broken down into glucose after ingestion or in metabolism, later.

In addition to heart attacks and lower-bowel disease, diets high in refined sugar and flour are directly or indirectly implicated in vitamin-deficiency diseases, obesity, tooth decay, gastric ulcers, indigestion, gall-bladder disease, hormone disorders, appendicitis, kidney stones, urinary-tract infections, and pelvic congestion leading to varicose veins, hemorrhoids, and leg-vein thrombosis (clotting obstruction). They also create havoc with the metabolic balance of those who suffer from diabetes, or its opposite, hypoglycemia, with all its related mental and emotional symptoms.

If all of these were not enough, here's one more problem: If sugar (in any form) is not burned up by adequate exercise, it is converted to fat, which is not only deposited or stored under the skin, but also in the liver and around many other internal organs, and worst of all, along the inner lining of the arteries. This, together with a rise in blood cholesterol caused by excess dietary sugar, leads to arteriosclerosis, or narrowing of the major arterial blood vessels. The most vulnerable of these, the very first branch off the ascending aorta, is the main coronary artery supplying the heart itself. Hence the direct indictment of ingested white sugar to the everincreasing occurrences of heart attacks in those who are overweight and overfed, but malnourished and underexercised.

Appendix F
The Six-Hour
Glucose-Tolerance Test

THE NORMAL BLOOD-SUGAR LEVEL is usually maintained between 80 and 120 mgs per 100 cc, and in the healthy person this neither rises much higher after a high-carbohydrate meal nor falls much lower after the usual twelve-hour fast from 7:00 P.M. to 7:00 A.M. Controlled quantities of insulin, released by the pancreas after a meal, cause any excess glucose to be stored in the liver and muscles, in the form of glycogen. This, in turn, is broken down again to glucose, during the night hours, to prevent the level from falling too low.

In the glucose-tolerance test, a drink containing 100 grams of glucose is given after a fast of several hours, and blood samples are taken from a vein at hourly intervals. The expected initial rise in blood glucose level during the first hour or two should soon start coming down to below 120 mgs. (If it does not, the patient probably has diabetes.) The important levels for the suspected hypoglycemia victim are those taken at the fifth and sixth hours after drinking the glucose. If the level falls below 80 mgs and keeps on falling, too much insulin is being produced, and hypoglycemia is the probable diagnosis.

Appendix G
Sources of Essential Vitamins

Vitamin A (retinol) is necessary for healthy skin and clear vision, especially at nighttime. It can be reduced by stress in any form. It is available in plenty in fish-liver oil, liver, giblets, apricots, carrots, yellow squash, egg yolk, butter, and cream.

Vitamin B complex is most widely available in liver, legumes, potatoes, nuts, brewer's yeast, and, best of all, wheat germ. Eggs and pork are also good sources.

Vitamin B_1 (thiamine) is necessary for heart-muscle and nerve-cell function, and deficiency is known to lead to the disease beriberi, once common in Far Eastern countries, in communities subsisting on polished rice.

Vitamin B_2 (riboflavin), found in milk, cheese, meat, liver, and eggs, is important in protein metabolism; a deficiency leads to skin and eye problems.

Vitamin B_6 (pyridoxine) is found in yeast, liver, fish, legumes, and whole-grain cereals, and is needed for amino- and fatty-acid metabolism. Deficiency can cause diseases of blood, skin, and nerves.

Niacin (nicotinic acid), found with other B-complex vitamins, is needed in carbohydrate metabolism, and its deficiency leads to the disease of pellagra, common in some areas of India. It is marked by skin eruptions and digestive and nervous disorders.

Vitamin B_{12} (cobalamin) is found richly in meats and liver; if deficient, it can lead to *anemia* or "tired blood."

Other important members of the B complex are pantothenic acid, biotin, folic acid, choline, inositol, rutin and para-amino benzoic acid.

Vitamin C (ascorbic acid) helps guard against many infections and the chemical pollutants assaulting us from the air, water, and processed foods. It is an essential ingredient in healing of wounds, especially in bones and blood vessels. It becomes increasingly important in advancing age as a general defense, and throughout life it acts as a control on the reproduction of the common cold virus we're all liable to suffer. Recent research also suggests that Vitamin C can reduce cholesterol build-up within small arteries and thereby contribute to protecting against heart disease.

Almost all fruits and vegetables, particularly those of the citrus variety or their fresh juices, are high in Vitamin C. Especially good, also, are tomatoes, potatoes, cabbage, and green peppers. A serious deficiency disease, scurvy, used to afflict sailors deprived of fresh fruit on long voyages. Physicians in the eighteenth-century British Navy discovered that large supplies of oranges, tangerines, grapefruits, lemons, and limes prevented scurvy in their crews. Hence, in 1780 the newly free Americans used to call the English *limeys!*

Vitamin D (calciferol) is needed in the absorption and utilization of calcium and phosphorus, which are essential for the strengthening and repair of the bones. Deficiency leads to the bone diseases of rickets in children or osteomalacia in adults. Fish-liver oil, liver, egg yolk, and butter are rich sources, though the body can manufacture some when exposed to the ultraviolet radiation of sunlight.

Vitamin E (tocopherol), available in wheat germ, vegetable oil, egg yolk, legumes, and margarine, seems to be protective of a variety of cardiovascular disorders, enables wounds to heal more quickly, and contributes to tissue health in lungs and skin. Deficiency can lead to breakdown in the red blood cells.

Vitamin K is available in leafy vegetables and their oils and in pork liver; it is also manufactured in the intestine by intestinal bacteria, after the fourth day of life. It is essential for the formation of prothrombin, vital for normal blood clotting. Deficiency leads to bleeding disease. It is of interest that modern science has discovered that the concentrations of Vitamin K and prothrombin in newborn infants are at their highest on the eighth day. That is exactly the day when God ordered His chosen people, four thousand years ago, to circumcise their male offspring, the very day when hemorrhage was least likely.

Let me just mention the essential minerals. They are calcium, phosphorus, magnesium, iron, zinc, copper, iodine, manganese, molybdenum, chromium, and selenium. All are available in a balanced diet of natural foods, but all can be supplemented along with vitamins in tablet or liquid form. These can usually be available without prescription from a pharmacy or a health-food store.

Do some reading on the subject. The whole science of nutrition in health is fascinating.

Appendix H

The Stress of Adjusting
to Change

DOCTORS THOMAS HOLMES AND RICHARD RAHE, psychiatrists at the University of Washington devised this scale of stressful events based on average responses to very extensive interviews and questionnaires given to hundreds of men and women of varying ages, backgrounds and classes. On a scale of zero to one hundred the people responding were told that marriage was to be ranked at fifty.

Death of spouse headed the list, and it was later found that this stress resulted in ten times as many deaths in the widows and widowers as in a control group of the same age during the first year after bereavement. Similarly, divorced persons were twelve times more vulnerable to illness in the year following divorce than married people of equivalent age.

This stress scale remember is not all negative. Many good things can also stress you, like winning the state lottery, inheriting a fortune, falling in love, winning an election, and, most significant, becoming a born-again or Spirit-filled Christian. These particular events are not in this scale; but see where you would place them!

Events	Scale of Impact
Death of spouse	100
Divorce	73
Marital separation	65
Jail term	63
Death of close family member	63
Personal injury or illness	53
Marriage	50

Events	Scale of Impact
Fired at work	47
Marital reconciliation	45
Retirement	45
Change in health of family member	44
Pregnancy	40
Sex difficulties	39
Gain of new family member	39
Business readjustment	39
Change in financial state	38
Death of close friend	37
Change to different line of work	36
Change in number of arguments with spouse	35
Mortgage over $10,000	31
Foreclosure of mortgage or loan	30
Change in responsibilities at work	29
Son or daughter leaving home	29
Trouble with in-laws	29
Outstanding personal achievement	28
Wife begins or stops work	26
Begin or end school	26
Change in living conditions	25
Revision of personal habits	24
Trouble with boss	23
Change in work hours or conditions	20
Change in residence	20
Change in schools	20
Change in recreation	19
Change in church activities	19
Change in social activities	18
Mortgage or loan less than $10,000	17
Change in sleeping habits	16
Change in number of family get-togethers	15
Change in eating habits	15
Vacation	13
Christmas	12
Minor violations of the law	11

Appendix I

Eight Sports:
How Much They Help What

ACCORDING TO JAMES FIXX, in his book on running, seven exercise experts were asked by the President's Council on Physical Fitness and Sports to rank eight popular forms of exercise. Each panelist could award each sport anything from zero to three (maximum benefit) in each of nine effects on fitness and well-being. Here are the additions of all seven panelists' scores (21 being the highest possible score).

	Run-ning	Bicy-cling	Swim-ming	Hand-Ball or Squash	Ten-nis	Walk-ing	Golf	Bowl-ing
Physical Fitness								
Cardio-respiratory endurance	21	19	21	19	16	13	8	5
Muscular endurance	20	18	20	18	16	14	8	5
Muscular strength	17	16	14	15	14	11	9	5
Flexibility	9	9	15	16	14	7	8	7
Balance	17	18	12	17	16	8	8	6
General Well-Being								
Weight control	21	20	15	19	16	13	6	5
Muscle definition	14	15	14	11	13	11	6	5
Digestion	13	12	13	13	12	11	7	7
Sleep	16	15	16	12	11	14	6	6
TOTAL	148	142	140	140	128	102	66	51

Appendix J

Calorific Expenditures of Various Activities

THESE ARE the approximate number of calories expended per minute, per ten minutes, and per hour, for an average 170-pound man. Reduce by 20 percent for an average 130-pound woman. Also see Appendix K for a more detailed chart on expenditures in running, based on body weight and pace.

	CALORIFIC EXPENDITURE		
Activity	*Per Minute*	*Per Ten Minutes*	*Per Hour*
Sleeping	1	10	60
Sitting and talking	1.25	12.5	75
Standing	1.5	15	90
Strolling at less than two mph; light housework; gardening; raking leaves	2	20	120
Walking three mph; cycling six mph; bowling; cleaning windows, mopping floors, vacuuming; mowing grass; horseback riding	4	40	240
Table tennis; fencing; volleyball; tennis, squash, racquetball or badminton doubles; golf (carrying own clubs); calisthenics; ballet exercises; modern dance; scrubbing floors; shoveling snow	5	50	300
Walking four mph; cycling ten mph; ice or roller skating for fun; baseball; softball; gymnastics	6	60	360
Walking five mph; cycling eleven mph; tennis, racquetball singles	7	70	420
Jogging five mph; cycling twelve mph; running in place; swimming breast stroke laps nonstop; badminton singles	8	80	480
Jogging six mph, cycling fourteen mph; basketball; squash or handball singles; downhill skiing; competitive ice or roller skating	11	110	660
Running seven mph; boxing or wrestling; swimming crawl stroke. (Seven mph is just over eight and a half minutes per mile; a good running pace for those past thirty-five)	13	130	780

CALORIFIC EXPENDITURE

Activity	Per Minute	Per Ten Minutes	Per Hour
Running eight mph; skipping rope. (Eight mph is seven and a half minutes per mile; a good aim for those under thirty-five)	15	150	900
Race rowing; cross-country skiing; running ten mph	19	190	1,140
Marathon winner (26.2 miles in two hours ten minutes or over twelve mph)	23	230	1,380

Appendix K

Calorific Cost of Running

CALORIES USED PER MINUTE OF RUNNING

Weight (In pounds)	Pace Per Mile (In Minutes and Seconds)								
	5:20	6:00	6:40	7:20	8:00	8:40	9:20	10:00	10:40
120	15.6	13.8	12.1	10.9	9.9	9.0	8.3	7.6	7.0
130	16.9	14.8	13.2	11.8	10.7	9.7	8.9	8.2	7.6
140	18.1	15.9	14.1	12.6	11.5	10.5	9.6	8.8	8.1
150	19.4	17.0	15.1	13.5	12.3	11.2	10.2	9.4	8.7
160	20.6	18.1	16.1	14.5	13.0	11.8	10.9	10.0	9.3
170	21.9	19.2	17.0	15.3	13.8	12.7	11.5	10.6	9.8
180	23.1	20.2	18.0	16.2	14.6	13.3	12.2	11.2	10.4
190	24.4	21.3	19.0	17.0	15.4	14.0	12.9	11.8	10.9
200	25.6	22.4	19.9	17.9	16.2	14.8	13.5	12.4	11.5
210	26.9	23.6	20.9	18.7	17.0	15.5	14.1	13.0	12.1
220	28.1	24.7	21.9	19.6	17.8	16.2	14.8	13.6	12.6

CALORIES USED PER MILE OF RUNNING

Weight (In pounds)	Pace Per mile (In Minutes and Seconds)								
	5:20	6:00	6:40	7:20	8:00	8:40	9:20	10:00	10:40
120	83	83	81	80	79	78	77	76	75
130	90	89	88	87	85	84	83	82	81
140	97	95	94	93	92	91	89	88	87
150	103	102	101	99	98	97	95	94	93
160	110	109	107	106	104	103	101	100	99
170	117	115	113	112	111	109	107	106	105
180	123	121	120	119	117	115	114	112	111
190	130	128	127	125	123	121	120	118	117
200	137	135	133	131	129	128	126	124	123
210	143	141	139	137	136	134	132	130	129
220	150	148	146	144	142	140	138	136	135

Remember: Expenditure of every 3,500 calories in excess of body's calorific intake equals a weight loss of one pound.

Appendix L

Contraindications to Strenuous Exercise

THERE ARE SOME, fortunately rare, medical conditions which would preclude strenuous exercise. You *must* ask your family physician about these if you have any known symptoms which you suspect might endanger you with much-increased activity. These conditions include:

1. Acute or severe chronic disorders of the heart's condition, efficiency, or rhythm.
2. Blockage (thrombosis or embolism), narrowing (stenosis or sclerosis) or weakening (aneurysm) of major blood vessels.
3. High diastolic blood pressure (lower figure, heart at rest), above 105 mm Hg.

4. Need for fixed-rate pacemakers.
5. Taking medications affecting heart rate, such as digitalis.
6. Any angina (heart pain across the front of the chest).
7. Severe shortness of breath from any disease of the lungs.
8. Acute infections or fevers such as influenza or those of the upper or lower respiratory tract.
9. Anemia of any cause.
10. Any serious blood chemical imbalance.
11. Uncontrolled diabetes.
12. Toxic or hypoactive thyroid or other serious endocrine disorder.
13. Pregnancy at thirty-five to forty weeks. (A woman in the earlier weeks of uncomplicated pregnancy may exercise lightly.)
14. Toxemia of pregnancy.
15. Kidney disease such as nephritis.
16. Liver disease such as hepatitis.
17. Serious acute or chronic muscular, arthritic, or bone disorders.
18. Marked obesity (over fifty pounds above average for height and frame).
19. Certain other uncontrolled metabolic disorders.
20. Overt psychotic conditions with reality-contact loss.

Scripture Index

Recommended Reading

Abrahamson, E. M. and Pezet, A. W. *Body, Mind, and Sugar.* New York: Holt, Rinehart and Winston, Inc., 1951.

Benson, Herbert. *The Relaxation Response.* New York: William Morrow & Co., 1975.

Berkow, Robert, ed. *The Merck Manual of Diagnosis and Therapy.* 13th ed. Rahway, NJ: Merck Co., 1977.

Cheraskin, E. *Psychodietetics.* Briarcliff Manor, NY: Stein and Day, 1974.

Cooper, Kenneth H. *Aerobics.* New York: Bantam Books, 1972.

Cooper, Kenneth H. *The Aerobics Way.* New York: M. Evans & Co., 1977.

Duffy, William. *Sugar Blues.* New York: Warner Books, 1976.

Field, Frank. *Take It Off With Frank.* New York: William Morrow & Co., 1978.

Fixx, James F. *The Complete Book of Running.* New York: Random House, 1977.

Germann, Donald R. *Too Young to Die.* New York: Farnsworth Publishing Co., 1974.

Gilmore, Haydn. *Jog for Your Life.* Grand Rapids, MI: Zondervan Corp., 1974.

Glasser, William. *Positive Addiction.* New York: Harper & Row, 1976.

Glover, Bob, and Shepherd, Jack. *The Runner's Handbook.* New York: Penguin Books, 1978.

Henderson, Joe. *Jog, Run, Race.* Mountain View, CA: World Publications, 1977.

Higdon, Hal. *Fitness After Forty.* Mountain View, CA: World Publications, 1974.

Hoyt, Creig, et al. *Food for Fitness.* Mountain View, CA: World Publications, 1975.

Hunter, Frances. *God's Answer to Fat: Lose It.* Houston, Texas: Hunter Ministries, 1976.

Kostrubala, Thaddeus. *The Joy of Running.* Philadelphia: J. B. Lippincott Co., 1976.

Lance, Kathryn. *Running for Health and Beauty: A Complete Guide for Women.* New York: Bobbs-Merrill, 1977.

Lovett, C. S. *Help Lord—The Devil Wants Me Fat.* Baldwin Park, CA: Personal Christianity, 1977.

Moore, Peter C. *"What's Wrong With Marijuana?"* Cincinnati, Ohio: Forward Movement Publications, 1978.

Selye, Hans. *Stress Without Distress.* Philadelphia: J. B. Lippincott, 1974.

Sheehan, George A. *Doctor Sheehan on Running.* Mountain View, CA: World Publications, 1975.

Sheehan, George. *Running and Being.* New York: Simon and Schuster, 1978.

Small, Dwight. H. *Christian: Celebrate Your Sexuality.* Old Tappan, NJ: Fleming H. Revell Co., 1974.

Smedes, Lewis B. *Sex for Christians.* Grand Rapids, MI: Wm. B. Eerdmans Publishing Co., 1976.

Trobisch, Walter. *My Beautiful Feeling.* Downers Grove, IL: Inter-Varsity Press, 1976.

Ullyot, Joan. *Women's Running.* Mountain View, CA: World Publications, 1976.

U.S. Government. *Food Is More Than Just Something to Eat.* Pueblo, CO: Nutrition.

White, John. *Eros Defiled: the Christian and Sexual Sin.* Downers Grove, IL: Inter-Varsity Press, 1977.

Periodicals

Executive Fitness, Rodale Press, Inc., 33 East Minor Street, Emmaus, PA 18049.

Executive Health, Pickfair Building, Rancho Santa Fe, CA 92067.

Prevention Magazine, Rodale Press, Inc., 33 East Minor Street, Emmaus, PA 18049.

Racquet Magazine, 342 Madison Avenue, New York, NY 10017.

Runner's World Magazine, P.O. Box 366, Mountain View, CA 94042.

Running Times, 12808 Occoquan Road, Woodbridge, VA 22192.

The Health Letter, P.O. Box 326, San Antonio, TX 78292.

The Jogger, National Jogging Association, 191 18th Street NW, Suite 830, Washington, DC 20006.